AVR Microcontroller Prog

Getting Started with the **AVR** in C++ for Beginners

First Edition
Sarful Hassan

Preface

Welcome to *AVR Microcontroller Programming*! This book provides a beginner-friendly introduction to AVR microcontrollers, helping you gain essential skills in programming and electronics. Whether you're starting from scratch or looking to enhance your knowledge, this book bridges the gap between theory and hands-on practice.

Who This Book Is For

This book is perfect for:

- Students and engineers exploring microcontrollers.
- Hobbyists and makers working on AVR-based projects.
- Educators teaching microcontroller programming.
- Anyone eager to dive into the world of AVR.

No prior microcontroller experience is needed, but basic programming and electronics knowledge will help.

How This Book Is Organized

The book includes:

1. An introduction to the AVR family.
2. Basics of AVR architecture and tools setup.
3. Digital and analog I/O concepts.
4. Step-by-step programming techniques.
5. Advanced topics like communication and power management.

Chapters include examples, diagrams, and exercises to make learning interactive and practical.

What Was Left Out

To keep it beginner-focused, advanced topics like real-time operating systems and complex assembly language are excluded.

Code Style (About the Code)

Code examples in C are simple, well-commented, and easy to follow. You can download them from **mechatronicslab.net** for hands-on practice.

Release Notes
This is the first edition, focused on AVR basics. Future updates will include advanced examples based on your feedback.

MechatronicsLAB Online Learning
Visit **mechatronicslab.net** for:

- Video tutorials and online courses.
- Project ideas and free resources.

For queries, contact **mechatronicslab@gmail.com**.

Acknowledgments for the First Edition
Thanks to the MechatronicsLAB team, my students, and my family for their unwavering support and inspiration.

Copyright
© MechatronicsLAB. Reproduction is prohibited without permission. Contact **mechatronicslab@gmail.com** for inquiries.

Disclaimer
Every effort has been made to ensure accuracy, but the author and publisher are not liable for errors. Use responsibly and refer to additional resources as needed.

Enjoy your journey into AVR microcontroller programming!

Table of Contents

Chapter-1 intro AVR Family 5

Chapter-2 AVR Architecture and Internal Components 9

Chapter-3 Setting Up the AVR Development Environment....25

Chapter-4 Digital I/O 32

Chapter-5 Analog I/O 45

Chapter-6 Advanced I/O 58

Chapter-7 Variables and Constants 68

Chapter-8 Data Types 77

Chapter-9 Data Type Conversion 87

Chapter-10 Control Structures 96

Chapter-11 Arithmetic Operators 108

Chapter-12 Boolean Operators.................................117

Chapter-13 Compound Operators 124

Chapter-14 Math...138

Chapter-15 Characters 150

Chapter-16 Communication 159

Chapter-17 Bluetooth Communication 167

Chapter-18 Functions 171

Chapter-19 Variable Scope 179

Chapter-20 Memory Management and EEPROM 187

Chapter-21 Power Management and Optimization 197

Chapter-1 intro AVR Family

1.1 What is a Microcontroller?
Definition and Core Functions

- **Explanation of Microcontrollers as Compact Computing Devices**
    - Microcontrollers are single-chip computers integrating a CPU, memory, input/output (I/O) ports, and peripherals such as timers, analog-to-digital converters (ADCs), and communication interfaces. This all-in-one design enables them to handle dedicated tasks in real-time.
- **Core Functions of Microcontrollers**
    - **CPU (Central Processing Unit)**: Executes instructions to perform computations and control.
    - **Memory**: Includes both RAM (for data) and Flash or ROM (for storing program code).
    - **I/O Ports**: Interfacing with external devices such as sensors, actuators, and displays.
    - **Peripherals**: Built-in modules like timers, ADCs, PWM generators, and communication interfaces (SPI, UART, I2C).

Differences Between Microcontrollers and Microprocessors
- **Key Distinctions**
    - **Microcontrollers** are self-contained, optimized for control-oriented applications with integrated peripherals, while **microprocessors** require external memory and peripherals, typically used in general-purpose computing (e.g., PCs).
    - Microcontrollers are optimized for low power and low cost, making them ideal for embedded systems where dedicated tasks need real-time execution.

- **Typical Use Cases**
  - Microcontrollers: Home automation, automotive electronics, industrial control systems, consumer gadgets.
  - Microprocessors: Desktop computers, laptops, servers.

Applications of Microcontrollers

- **Overview of Application Areas**
  - **Consumer Electronics**: Used in appliances, remote controls, toys, and personal electronics.
  - **Automotive**: Essential in engine control, ABS, infotainment, and airbag systems.
  - **Industrial Control**: Control systems in automation, robotics, and machinery.
  - **Internet of Things (IoT)**: Widely used in IoT devices, enabling connectivity, data collection, and control.

1.2 Introduction to the AVR Microcontroller Family
History and Evolution of AVR

- **Development of AVR by Atmel (now Microchip Technology)**
  - AVR microcontrollers were developed by Atmel in the mid-1990s, specifically optimized with RISC (Reduced Instruction Set Computing) architecture to achieve high-performance, low-power operation.
  - AVR's design has had a significant impact on embedded applications and is widely used in various fields, especially among hobbyists and in the maker community.
- **AVR's Role in Embedded Applications and Maker Community**
  - Known for their ease of use, AVR microcontrollers became highly popular in DIY electronics and education, partly due to their use in Arduino boards.

Different Families in the AVR Series

- **Core AVR Families**
  - **ATtiny**: Ultra-small, low-power devices suited for basic control applications with limited memory and I/O.
  - **ATmega**: Most commonly used family with a balance of memory, performance, and peripherals, used in Arduino boards and other general-purpose applications.
  - **ATxmega**: High-performance family with advanced peripherals, large memory options, and high-speed processing, ideal for demanding embedded applications.
- **Comparison of Key Features**
  - ATtiny: Compact, power-efficient, ideal for low-cost, simple applications.
  - ATmega: General-purpose, well-balanced for a variety of applications.
  - ATxmega: Advanced processing with extended memory and peripherals.

Advantages of Using AVR Microcontrollers

- **Benefits of RISC Architecture**
  - AVR microcontrollers use RISC architecture, allowing fast instruction execution and efficiency, making them well-suited for real-time embedded systems.
- **Ease of Programming and Community Support**
  - AVR microcontrollers are easy to program, with support for multiple programming languages (C/C++, Assembly) and a strong community with resources, libraries, and tutorials.
- **Key Advantages**
  - Fast processing, low power consumption, wide peripheral integration, and extensive tool and community support.

1.3 Applications of AVR Microcontrollers

Consumer Electronics and Home Automation

- **Examples in Gadgets and Appliances**
  - AVR microcontrollers are commonly used in devices like washing machines, microwave ovens, thermostats, and remote-controlled systems.
  - In home automation, AVRs control lighting, heating, security systems, and other smart home functions.

Industrial and Automotive Applications

- **Examples in Process Control and Robotic Systems**
  - AVR microcontrollers are utilized in industrial control systems for motor control, sensor data processing, and automation tasks.
  - In automotive electronics, they are used for engine control, dashboard displays, and other electronic control units (ECUs).

DIY and Maker Projects

- **Popularity in the Maker Community**
  - AVR-based Arduino boards sparked a global maker movement, enabling students, hobbyists, and engineers to create DIY electronics projects easily.
  - Examples of popular DIY projects include robotic arms, environmental sensors, home automation devices, and IoT prototypes.

Chapter-2 AVR Architecture and Internal Components

2.1 AVR CPU Architecture and Processing
RISC Architecture and Efficiency

- **Explanation of Reduced Instruction Set Computing (RISC)**
  - The AVR microcontrollers use a RISC architecture, meaning they are built with a limited number of simple instructions that can be executed quickly. This design enables faster processing and lower power consumption, as most instructions are executed in a single cycle.
- **Overview of 8-bit and 32-bit AVR Architectures**
  - The AVR family includes both 8-bit and 32-bit microcontrollers, but most popular models, like the ATmega and ATtiny, are 8-bit. These are optimized for low-power and embedded applications, with 32-bit models available for more advanced needs.

Instruction Set and Execution Cycles

- **Brief Overview of the AVR Instruction Set**
  - AVR microcontrollers have a compact instruction set, including data transfer, arithmetic, logic, and control instructions. This simplicity allows rapid code execution and minimal clock cycles per instruction.
- **Single-Cycle Execution**
  - Most instructions execute in a single cycle, improving response time and efficiency in embedded applications.

2.2 Registers and Special Function Registers (SFRs)
General Purpose Registers

- **Overview of 32 General-Purpose Registers (R0-R31)**
  - AVR microcontrollers feature 32 general-purpose registers (R0-R31) that serve as quick-access data storage for calculations and intermediate values.
  - **Register Pairs for 16-Bit Operations**: Registers can be paired (e.g., R24 and R25) for 16-bit data handling, which is essential for larger data operations and efficient memory manipulation.

Special Function Registers (SFRs)

- **Key SFRs for Peripheral Control**
  - Special Function Registers (SFRs) control various peripherals and functionalities of the microcontroller. Notable SFRs include:
    - **TCCR (Timer Control Registers)**: Used for configuring timers.
    - **PORT**: Manages the I/O pins.
    - **ADMUX (ADC Multiplexer)**: Selects input channels for analog-to-digital conversions.
  - These SFRs allow direct control over AVR microcontroller functions and hardware interfaces.

2.3 Memory Organization in AVR Microcontrollers
Program Memory (Flash)

- **Explanation of Flash Memory for Code Storage**
  - AVR microcontrollers use Flash memory to store program code, allowing data to remain even when the power is off. Flash also supports a bootloader, enabling firmware updates without an external programmer.
  - Flash memory is accessed using the program counter (PC), which points to the address of the instruction to be executed.

Data Memory (SRAM and EEPROM)

- **SRAM for Runtime Data Storage**
  - SRAM (Static Random Access Memory) is used to store temporary data, such as variables and function parameters, during program execution. SRAM is volatile, meaning its data is lost when the microcontroller is powered off.
- **EEPROM for Non-Volatile Data**
  - EEPROM (Electrically Erasable Programmable Read-Only Memory) is used for data that must be retained after power loss, such as calibration values, configuration settings, and user preferences.

Memory Map and Addressing Modes

- **Linear Memory Map**
  - AVR microcontrollers have a linear memory map that provides straightforward access across memory regions, simplifying data handling and program control.
- **Common Addressing Modes**
  - AVR supports several addressing modes, such as:
    - **Direct Addressing**: Accessing specific memory locations.
    - **Indirect Addressing**: Accessing memory using pointer registers.
  - These modes enable efficient data access and manipulation in embedded applications.

2.4 Input/Output Ports and Peripheral Control
Digital I/O with PORT and DDR Registers

- **Configuring I/O Pins as Input or Output**
  - The Data Direction Register (DDR) configures each I/O pin as either an input or output:
    - **DDR = 1**: Configures the pin as an output.
    - **DDR = 0**: Configures the pin as an input.

- **Controlling Data with PORT Registers**
    - The PORT register manages the state of output pins and enables pull-up resistors on input pins. Writing to PORT toggles pin values, useful for applications like LED control.

Analog Inputs and PWM Outputs

- **Analog-to-Digital Conversion (ADC) in AVR**
    - Many AVR microcontrollers feature ADCs, which convert analog signals (e.g., from sensors) into digital values. Configured using registers like ADMUX, ADCs enable precise monitoring of analog inputs for embedded applications.
- **Pulse-Width Modulation (PWM) Output**
    - PWM is generated by configuring timers and setting output pins to modulate signal width. Commonly used for controlling motors, LEDs, and audio signals, PWM adjusts the duty cycle to vary output power.

2.5 ATMEGA32 Pin Configuration

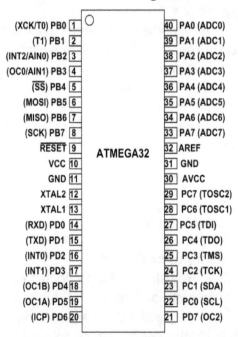

Pin No.	Pin Name	Description	Alternate Function
1	PB0 (XCK/T0)	Pin 0 of PORTB	T0: Timer0 External Counter Input, XCK: USART Clock I/O
2	PB1 (T1)	Pin 1 of PORTB	T1: Timer1 External Counter Input
3	PB2 (INT2/AIN0)	Pin 2 of PORTB	INT2: External Interrupt 2, AIN0: Analog Comparator
4	PB3 (OC0/AIN1)	Pin 3 of PORTB	OC0: Timer0 Output Compare Match, AIN1: Analog Comparator Negative
5	PB4 (SS)	Pin 4 of PORTB	SS: SPI Slave Select
6	PB5 (MOSI)	Pin 5 of PORTB	MOSI: SPI Master Output, Slave Input
7	PB6 (MISO)	Pin 6 of PORTB	MISO: SPI Master Input, Slave Output
8	PB7 (SCK)	Pin 7 of PORTB	SCK: SPI Serial Clock
9	RESET	Active Low Reset Pin	Pulled HIGH for RESET

10	Vcc	Power Supply	+5V
11	GND	Ground	-
12, 13	XTAL2, XTAL1	Connected to Crystal Oscillator	-
14	PD0 (RXD)	Pin 0 of PORTD	RXD: USART Input
15	PD1 (TXD)	Pin 1 of PORTD	TXD: USART Output
16-21	PD2 to PD7	Pins of PORTD for external interrupts and PWM channels	INT0, INT1, OC1B, OC1A, ICP, OC2
22, 23	PC0 (SCL), PC1 (SDA)	TWI Interface	For Two-Wire Serial Communication
24-27	PC2 to PC5	JTAG Interface Pins	TCK, TMS, TDO, TDI
28, 29	PC6, PC7	Timer Oscillator Pins	TOSC1, TOSC2
30	AVcc	ADC Power Supply	+5V
31	GND	Ground	-

32	AREF	ADC Reference Voltage	-
33-40	PA0 to PA7	ADC Channels (Analog to Digital Converter)	ADC Channels 0 to 7

ATMEGA32 Features
1. **CPU Architecture:** 8-bit AVR.
2. **I/O Pins:** 32 programmable I/O pins.
3. **Communication Interfaces:**
   - USART
   - SPI
   - TWI (I^2C)
   - JTAG
4. **Memory:**
   - Flash: 32 KB
   - SRAM: 2 KB
   - EEPROM: 1 KB
5. **ADC:** 8 channels, 10-bit resolution.
6. **PWM Channels:** 4 PWM outputs.
7. **Timers:**
   - Two 8-bit timers.
   - One 16-bit timer.
8. **Clock Speeds:**
   - Internal Oscillator: 0-8 MHz.
   - External Oscillator: 0-16 MHz.
9. **Watchdog Timer:** Programmable with separate on-chip oscillator.
10. **Power Modes:** Six modes for power saving.

2.6 Comparison of ATMEGA32 with Other AVR Microcontrollers

Feature	ATMEGA32	ATMEGA16	ATMEGA328P	ATMEGA8
Architecture	8-bit AVR	8-bit AVR	8-bit AVR	8-bit AVR
Program Memory	32 KB Flash	16 KB Flash	32 KB Flash	8 KB Flash
RAM	2 KB	1 KB	2 KB	1 KB
EEPROM	1 KB	512 Bytes	1 KB	512 Bytes
Operating Voltage	4.5 - 5.5V	4.5 - 5.5V	1.8 - 5.5V	4.5 - 5.5V
Clock Speed	16 MHz (max)	16 MHz (max)	20 MHz (max)	16 MHz (max)
ADC	8 channels, 10-bit	8 channels, 10-bit	6 channels, 10-bit	6 channels, 10-bit
Timers	2 × 8-bit, 1 × 16-bit	2 × 8-bit, 1 × 16-bit	2 × 8-bit, 1 × 16-bit	2 × 8-bit, 1 × 16-bit
PWM Channels	4	4	6	3

Communication Interfaces	USART, SPI, TWI, JTAG	USART, SPI, TWI, JTAG	USART, SPI, TWI	USART, SPI, TWI
I/O Pins	32	32	23	23
Power Save Modes	6 modes	6 modes	6 modes	6 modes
Watchdog Timer	Yes	Yes	Yes	Yes
Applications	Advanced Embedded Systems, Control Systems	Medium-scale Systems	Portable Devices, IoT	Small Embedded Systems

Recommendations

- **ATMEGA32:** For advanced embedded systems with high memory and multiple peripherals.
- **ATMEGA16:** For budget-friendly medium-scale applications.
- **ATMEGA328P:** Best for portable and low-power devices like IoT systems.
- **ATMEGA8:** Ideal for beginners or small-scale embedded systems.

2.7 Exploration of ATMEGA32 Features

1. Analog Inputs

- **Technical Details:**
    - 8 ADC channels available (PA0 to PA7).
    - 10-bit resolution: Converts an analog input into a digital value ranging from 0 to 1023.
    - ADC Reference Voltage (AREF): Can be set externally or internally (AVcc or 2.56V reference).
    - Sampling Rate: Supports up to 15 K samples/second.
    - Single-ended or differential input with selectable gain.
- **How to Use:**
    - Configure ADC pins (PA0 to PA7) as input.
    - Set up the ADC control registers for voltage reference, prescaler, and channel selection.
    - Start conversion and read the digital value from the ADC Data Register (ADCL and ADCH).
- **Practical Example:**
    - Connect a temperature sensor like **LM35** to PA0.
    - Measure the voltage output (proportional to temperature).
    - Convert the voltage to temperature using a scaling factor.

---

2. PWM Outputs

- **Technical Details:**
    - 4 PWM channels:
        - OC0 (Timer0)
        - OC1A and OC1B (Timer1)
        - OC2 (Timer2)
    - Adjustable duty cycle (0-100%) using Timer/Counter compare registers.
    - Operates in various modes:
        - Fast PWM.
        - Phase Correct PWM.

- **How to Use:**
  - Configure the PWM pin as output.
  - Set up the corresponding timer in PWM mode (Fast or Phase Correct).
  - Adjust the duty cycle by modifying the compare match register (OCRx).
- **Practical Example:**
  - Use OC1A to control the speed of a DC motor by varying the duty cycle.
  - Use OC2 to dim an LED smoothly by ramping the PWM duty cycle from 0% to 100%.

---

3. USART (Universal Synchronous and Asynchronous Receiver-Transmitter)

- **Technical Details:**
  - Baud rate: Configurable for different communication speeds (e.g., 9600 bps).
  - Modes: Asynchronous, Synchronous, and Master SPI.
  - Data Format: Configurable for 5, 6, 7, 8, or 9-bit data packets with parity options.
  - Full duplex (simultaneous sending and receiving).
- **How to Use:**
  - Configure PD0 (RXD) and PD1 (TXD) for serial communication.
  - Set baud rate using the UBRR (USART Baud Rate Register).
  - Enable transmitter and receiver using control registers.
  - Use USART Data Register (UDR) to send and receive data.

- **Practical Example:**
    - Connect to a PC using a USB-to-serial adapter.
    - Send sensor data to the terminal for monitoring and debugging.
    - Use USART to control the microcontroller remotely by sending commands.

---

4. I²C (TWI - Two-Wire Interface)

- **Technical Details:**
    - Operates using SCL (PC0) and SDA (PC1) pins.
    - Supports master and slave modes.
    - Standard speed: 100 kHz, Fast speed: 400 kHz.
    - Supports 7-bit addressing for peripheral devices.
- **How to Use:**
    - Configure PC0 (SCL) and PC1 (SDA) as I²C pins.
    - Set the TWI control and status registers to enable the I²C module.
    - Use start, write, and read commands to communicate with peripherals.
- **Practical Example:**
    - Connect a temperature sensor (**DS18B20**) to measure ambient temperature.
    - Interface with an external EEPROM (e.g., **AT24C32**) to store sensor readings.

---

5. SPI (Serial Peripheral Interface)

- **Technical Details:**
    - Operates in full-duplex mode.
    - Pins:
        - MOSI (PB5): Master Out, Slave In.
        - MISO (PB6): Master In, Slave Out.
        - SCK (PB7): Clock Signal.
        - SS (PB4): Slave Select.
    - Data transmission: Configurable clock polarity and phase.

- **How to Use:**
  - Configure SPI control registers for master/slave mode and clock settings.
  - Use MOSI, MISO, SCK, and SS pins for data transmission.
  - Write data to the SPI Data Register (SPDR) and wait for the transmission to complete.
- **Practical Example:**
  - Interface with an **SD card** to log data (e.g., temperature, humidity).
  - Connect a graphical LCD to display real-time sensor data.

2.8 Power Supply for ATMEGA32

A stable and reliable power supply is critical for the proper functioning of the ATMEGA32 microcontroller. Below is a detailed guide on powering the ATMEGA32.

Voltage Requirements
- **Operating Voltage Range:**
  - **ATMEGA32 Standard Version:** 4.5V to 5.5V.
  - **ATMEGA32L (Low-Voltage Version):** 2.7V to 5.5V.
- **Recommended Voltage:** 5V for general applications.

Power Supply Pins
- **Vcc (Pin 10):** Primary power supply pin for the microcontroller core.
- **AVcc (Pin 30):** Power supply for the ADC (Analog-to-Digital Converter). It must be connected to the same voltage as Vcc (with proper decoupling capacitors) for ADC operations.
- **GND (Pins 11 and 31):** Ground pins.

Power Supply Circuit Design

1. Using a 5V Regulated Power Supply

- **Components Required:**
    1. Voltage Regulator (e.g., **7805** for 5V output).
    2. Input Capacitors (e.g., 10 µF and 0.1 µF).
    3. Output Capacitors (e.g., 10 µF and 0.1 µF).
    4. Diode (e.g., **1N4007**) for polarity protection.
- **Circuit Design Steps:**
    1. Use a 12V DC input (e.g., battery or adapter).
    2. Place a 1N4007 diode in series with the input to protect against reverse polarity.
    3. Connect the input to the **7805 voltage regulator**'s input pin.
    4. Place a 10 µF capacitor between the input pin and ground.
    5. Connect the output pin of the regulator to the Vcc pin of the ATMEGA32.
    6. Place a 10 µF capacitor between the output pin and ground.
    7. Optionally, use a 0.1 µF ceramic capacitor for noise suppression.

2. USB-Based Power Supply

- **Components Required:**
    1. USB Connector (5V supply from USB port).
    2. Capacitors for decoupling (10 µF and 0.1 µF).
    3. Diode (e.g., **1N4007**) for protection.
- **Steps:**
    1. Connect the Vcc and GND of the USB connector to the corresponding Vcc and GND of the ATMEGA32.
    2. Add a decoupling capacitor (10 µF) between Vcc and GND for stability.

3. Battery-Based Power Supply

- **Components Required:**
    1. Battery (e.g., 9V or 12V).
    2. Voltage Regulator (e.g., **7805** for 5V).
    3. Capacitors (10 µF and 0.1 µF).
- **Steps:**
    1. Connect the battery to the input of the 7805 voltage regulator.
    2. Use capacitors for stability and noise filtering.
    3. Connect the regulated 5V output to the Vcc of the ATMEGA32.

---

4. Power Supply Decoupling

- Always use decoupling capacitors (0.1 µF) near the Vcc and AVcc pins to minimize noise and improve stability.

Power Considerations

1. **Current Requirements:**
    - Ensure the power source can supply enough current for the ATMEGA32 and any peripherals connected.
    - Typical operating current: ~10-20 mA (without peripherals).
    - Maximum current: Depends on the connected load (e.g., LEDs, motors).
2. **ADC Performance:**
    - Connect **AVcc** to the same voltage as Vcc for proper ADC operation.
    - Use a low-pass filter (e.g., 10 µH inductor and 0.1 µF capacitor) on the AVcc line to reduce noise.
3. **Brown-Out Detection:**
    - ATMEGA32 includes a **Brown-Out Detector (BOD)** to reset the microcontroller if the voltage drops below a safe level.

4. **Sleep Modes:**
   - Use the microcontroller's sleep modes to reduce power consumption in battery-powered applications.

Example Power Supply Circuit
1. **12V DC Adapter Input:**
   - Use a 12V DC adapter connected to a 7805 voltage regulator.
   - Filter the input and output with capacitors.
   - Connect the regulated 5V to Vcc and AVcc pins.
2. **Battery-Based System:**
   - A 9V battery connected to a 7805 regulator provides stable 5V for Vcc.
   - Add decoupling capacitors for noise suppression.

2.9 Importance of a Proper Power Supply for ATMEGA32
Key Reasons Why a Proper Power Supply is Crucial:

- **Microcontroller Stability:**
  - Ensures consistent operation by preventing resets and glitches caused by voltage fluctuations.
- **ADC Accuracy:**
  - Stabilizes AVcc and AREF for precise analog-to-digital conversions, reducing noise and ensuring accurate sensor readings.
- **Reliable Communication:**
  - Prevents data corruption and ensures robust operation of USART, SPI, and I²C interfaces.
- **Brown-Out Prevention:**
  - Protects against unpredictable behavior by maintaining voltage above the operating threshold (4.5V for ATMEGA32).
- **Peripheral Functionality:**
  - Supports stable operation of LEDs, motors, and sensors without voltage drops affecting the microcontroller.

- **Hardware Protection:**
  - Protects the ATMEGA32 and peripherals from damage due to overvoltage or undervoltage.
- **Noise Reduction:**
  - Reduces interference from external devices through proper decoupling and filtering.
- **Efficient Sleep Modes:**
  - Enables proper activation of low-power modes to save energy in battery-powered applications.
- **Stable ADC and Timer Performance:**
  - Maintains consistent ADC readings and reliable PWM signals from timers by stabilizing AVcc.
- **System Efficiency:**
  - Minimizes energy loss, reduces heating, and optimizes battery life in portable systems.

Chapter-3 Setting Up the AVR Development Environment

3.1 Overview of AVR Development Tools
Software Tools: AVR Studio and Arduino IDE

- **Introduction to Atmel Studio (AVR Studio) for Advanced Development**
  - Atmel Studio, also known as AVR Studio, is a comprehensive IDE developed by Microchip for professional AVR development. It offers features such as debugging, simulation, and support for multiple AVR devices, making it ideal for advanced users and large projects.
- **Overview of Arduino IDE for Beginners and Makers**
  - The Arduino IDE is designed for ease of use, making it perfect for beginners and hobbyists. It provides a simplified coding environment and library support, allowing users to quickly develop and upload code to AVR-based boards like the Arduino Uno.

Hardware Tools for AVR Development

- **AVR ISP (In-System Programmer), USBasp, and Arduino as an ISP**
  - **AVR ISP**: A commonly used programmer for uploading code to AVR microcontrollers directly on the board.
  - **USBasp**: A budget-friendly USB programmer that supports various AVR devices.
  - **Arduino as ISP**: Allows an Arduino board to act as a programmer for other AVR devices, ideal for programming ATtiny chips and other small AVRs.
- **Popular AVR Development Boards**
  - **Arduino Uno**: Based on the ATmega328, this board is widely used for learning and prototyping in the maker community.
  - **ATtiny Boards**: Compact boards with ATtiny microcontrollers, useful for simple applications where space and power are limited.

3.2 Installing and Configuring Atmel Studio (AVR Studio)
Step 1: Downloading Atmel Studio

- Visit the official Microchip Studio download page.
- Select the installer compatible with your operating system.
- Save the installer file to your computer.

Step 2: Installing Atmel Studio

- Run the installer file and follow the installation wizard:
  - Accept the license agreement.
  - Choose the installation location (default or custom).
  - Select components (keep default options).
- Click "Install" and wait for the process to complete.
- Finish the installation and launch Atmel Studio.

Step 3: Setting Up the Development Environment

- Launch Atmel Studio.
- Create a new project:
  - Go to `File > New > Project`.
  - Select **AVR GCC** under "Installed Templates" and choose "C Executable Project."
  - Name the project and specify a location.
- Select the device:
  - Search for your microcontroller (e.g., ATMEGA32).
  - Click "OK" to finalize the setup.
- Configure the toolchain:
  - Open `Project > Properties`.
  - Under the "Toolchain" tab, set compiler options and debugging configurations.

Step 4: Connecting Hardware

- Install USB drivers for your programmer (e.g., USBasp, Atmel ICE).
- Connect the microcontroller using the programmer or debugger.
- Verify the connection:
  - Go to `Tools > Device Programming`.
  - Select the programmer and device, click "Apply," and then "Read" to verify communication.

Step 5: Writing and Compiling Code

- Write code in the editor for your AVR microcontroller.
- Build the project:
  - Click `Build > Build Solution` or press **F7**.
  - Check the output window for errors or warnings.
- Generate a HEX file:
  - The HEX file is located in the project's output directory (e.g., `\Debug\` or `\Release\`).

Step 6: Programming the Microcontroller

- Open the programming tool:
  - Go to Tools > Device Programming.
- Select the programmer and device.
- Load the HEX file:
  - Under "Memories," browse and load the HEX file generated during the build.
- Program the device:
  - Click "Program" and verify the success message.

Step 7: Debugging (Optional)

- Start debugging:
  - Go to Debug > Start Debugging and Break or press **F5**.
  - Use breakpoints to analyze code behavior.
- Simulate without hardware:
  - Use the built-in simulator for testing your program without connecting hardware.

Tips for Configuration

- Adjust optimization levels in the toolchain settings to balance speed and size.
- Enable debugging symbols for effective debugging.
- Install additional libraries or plugins for specific hardware (e.g., LCD, sensors).

Troubleshooting

- If the programmer is not detected, ensure drivers are installed and the correct COM port is selected.
- For compilation errors, check syntax or missing device-specific header files.
- Verify fuse bit settings and power supply for upload issues.
  -

Writing and Testing a Simple "Hello World" Program for ATMEGA32
Step 1: Setting Up the Project

- Open Atmel Studio.
- Create a new project:
    - Go to File > New > Project.
    - Select **AVR GCC > C Executable Project**.
    - Name the project (e.g., "HelloWorld") and click "OK."
- Select the target device:
    - Search for **ATMEGA32** in the device list.
    - Select it and click "OK."

Step 2: Writing the Code
Below is the "Hello World" program that toggles an LED connected to **PORTB0** of the ATMEGA32.

```
#define F_CPU 1000000UL    // Define the CPU frequency (1 MHz for
internal oscillator)
#include <avr/io.h>        // Include header file for I/O operations
#include <util/delay.h>    // Include header file for delay functions

int main(void) {
    // Set PORTB0 as output
    DDRB |= (1 << PB0);

    while (1) {
        // Toggle PORTB0
        PORTB ^= (1 << PB0);
        // Delay for 500 ms
        _delay_ms(500);
    }

    return 0; // Optional, microcontroller does not return from main
}
```

Code Explanation:

1. #define F_CPU: Sets the clock frequency for the delay functions. Adjust based on your clock settings.
2. DDRB |= (1 << PB0): Configures **PORTB0** as an output pin.

3. `PORTB ^= (1 << PB0)`: Toggles the state of the LED connected to **PORTB0**.
4. `_delay_ms(500)`: Waits for 500 milliseconds to create a blinking effect.

Step 3: Compiling the Program

- Click on `Build > Build Solution` or press **F7**.
- Check the output window for any errors or warnings.
- Ensure the HEX file is generated in the project's output directory.

Step 4: Hardware Setup

- **Connections:**
  - Connect an LED to **PORTB0** (Pin 1 of ATMEGA32).
  - Use a 220-ohm resistor in series with the LED to limit current.
  - Provide a stable 5V power supply to Vcc and AVcc, and connect GND.
  - Connect the microcontroller to your programmer (e.g., USBasp).

Step 5: Programming the Microcontroller

- Open `Tools > Device Programming`.
- Select your programmer and ATMEGA32 as the target device.
- Click "Apply" to confirm settings.
- Under the "Memories" section:
  - Load the generated HEX file.
  - Click "Program" to upload the code to the microcontroller.

Step 6: Testing the Program

- Power on the circuit.
- The LED connected to **PORTB0** should blink with a 1-second cycle (500ms ON, 500ms OFF).

Troubleshooting Tips

- **LED Not Blinking:**
    - Ensure the LED polarity is correct (long leg to PORTB0, short leg to GND).
    - Check the resistor and power connections.
- **Program Not Uploading:**
    - Verify the programmer connections and drivers.
    - Ensure the correct device and HEX file are selected.
- **Incorrect Timing:**
    - Ensure the correct CPU frequency is defined (F_CPU).

Chapter-4 Digital I/O

Chapter Overview

Digital I/O (Input/Output) operations allow AVR microcontrollers to interface with external devices, such as LEDs, switches, and sensors. This chapter explains how to configure and use digital I/O pins on an AVR microcontroller using C in Atmel Studio. By the end of this chapter, you will understand how to control devices connected to the microcontroller and read input states.

Chapter Goal

- Learn how to configure AVR microcontroller pins as inputs or outputs.
- Understand how to control digital outputs and read digital inputs.
- Complete a project that uses a switch to control an LED, applying digital I/O concepts.

Rules

- **Pin Configuration**: Use the Data Direction Register (DDR) to set each pin's direction (input or output) before using it.
- **Port Registers**: Use DDRx, PORTx, and PINx registers to configure and read each pin's state.
- **Bitwise Operations**: Use bitwise operations (| =, &=, and ^=) for efficient pin control.
- **Internal Pull-Up Resistors**: Enable internal pull-up resistors for stable signal detection on input pins.

Brief Introduction to Registers (DDR, PORT, and PIN)

In AVR microcontrollers, the **DDR**, **PORT**, and **PIN** registers are fundamental for configuring and controlling digital I/O pins:

- **DDR (Data Direction Register)**: Controls the direction of each pin. Setting a bit to 1 configures the pin as an output, while setting it to 0 configures it as an input. Each port has its own DDR register, such as DDRB for Port B.

- **PORT Register**: Controls the output value of each pin. When a pin is set as an output, writing 1 to the corresponding bit in the PORT register sets the pin high, while writing 0 sets it low.
- **PIN Register**: Used to read the input value of each pin. When a pin is set as an input, the PIN register reflects the actual state (high or low) of each pin.

Brief Introduction to Pull-Up and Pull-Down Resistors

Pull-up and pull-down resistors are essential for stabilizing input signals:
- **Pull-Up Resistor**: Connects an input pin to a high voltage level through a resistor, ensuring that the pin reads high (1) when no external device drives it low. Internal pull-up resistors can be enabled on AVR microcontrollers by setting the pin to input and writing 1 to the corresponding PORT register bit.
- **Pull-Down Resistor**: Connects an input pin to ground through a resistor, ensuring the pin reads low (0) when no external device drives it high. AVR microcontrollers typically don't have internal pull-down resistors, so external pull-down resistors are used when needed.

Using pull-up and pull-down resistors prevents **floating** states, where an input pin reads unpredictable values.

Syntax Table

Serial No	Topic	Syntax	Simple Example
1	Set Entire Port as Output	DDRx = 0xFF;	DDRB = 0xFF;
2	Set Entire Port as Input	DDRx = 0x00;	DDRB = 0x00;

3	Set Individual Pin as Output	DDRx	= (1 << PinNo);
4	Set Individual Pin as Input	DDRx &= ~(1 << PinNo);	DDRB &= ~(1 << PB1);
5	Set Pin Output High	PORTx	= (1 << PinNo);
6	Set Pin Output Low	PORTx &= ~(1 << PinNo);	PORTB &= ~(1 << PB0);
7	Toggle Pin Output	PORTx ^= (1 << PinNo);	PORTB ^= (1 << PB0);
8	Read Individual Pin Input	int val = (PINx & (1 << PinNo));	int button = (PINB & (1 << PB1));

Topic Explanations

1. Set Entire Port as Output

What is Set Entire Port as Output

Setting an entire port as output enables all pins within that port to send signals simultaneously. This is useful when controlling multiple pins together, such as for LED arrays or displays.

Use Purpose

- **Multi-Output Configuration**: Quickly configures all pins in a port as outputs.
- **Efficient Control**: Controls multiple external devices with a single command.
- **Ideal for Large Arrays**: Used for driving LED arrays or similar output components.

Syntax

```
DDRx = 0xFF;
```

Syntax Explanation

- **DDRx**: The Data Direction Register for port x (e.g., DDRB for Port B).
    - **DDR Register**: Controls whether each pin is an input (0) or output (1).
    - Setting DDRx to 0xFF configures each pin in the port as an output.
- **0xFF**: Hexadecimal value representing all bits set to 1 (11111111 in binary).
    - This value sets all bits in DDRx to 1, configuring each pin in the port to output mode.

Simple Code Example

```
DDRB = 0xFF;  // Set all pins on Port B as output
```

Code Example Explanation

1. Accesses DDRB, the Data Direction Register for Port B.
2. Sets all bits to 1, configuring all pins in Port B as outputs.

Notes

- Configure only necessary ports as outputs to avoid interference with other devices.

Warnings

- Setting the entire port as output can affect other connected devices if they need certain pins as input.

---

2. Set Entire Port as Input

What is Set Entire Port as Input

Configuring an entire port as input allows each pin within that port to read external signals, useful for reading multiple input sources, such as switches or sensors.

Use Purpose

- **Multi-Input Setup**: Configures all pins in a port as inputs.
- **Ideal for Button Arrays**: Suitable for applications with multiple buttons or sensors.
- **Quick Configuration**: Sets up an entire port for input with a single command.

Syntax

```
DDRx = 0x00;
```

Syntax Explanation

- **DDRx**: The Data Direction Register for port x.
  - The **DDR** register specifies whether each pin in the port is an input or output.
  - Setting DDRx to 0x00 configures each pin as an input by setting each bit to 0.
- **0x00**: Hexadecimal value with all bits set to 0 (00000000 in binary).
  - By assigning 0x00 to DDRx, each pin is set to input mode, allowing external signals to be read.

Simple Code Example

```
DDRB = 0x00;  // Set all pins on Port B as input
```

Code Example Explanation

1. Accesses DDRB, the Data Direction Register for Port B.
2. Sets all bits in DDRB to 0, making each pin an input.

Notes

- Use internal pull-up resistors for stable inputs.

Warnings

- Floating inputs (pins with no connected signal) may cause unpredictable readings; use pull-ups if needed.

3. Set Individual Pin as Output

What is Set Individual Pin as Output

Configuring an individual pin as output enables only that specific pin to send signals, ideal for controlling single devices, like an LED or relay.

Use Purpose

- **Targeted Output Control**: Configures a single pin for output without affecting others.
- **Flexible Configuration**: Sets only the required pin as output, leaving other pins unaffected.
- **Multi-Functional Port Use**: Allows other pins within the same port to be configured as input or output.

Syntax

```
DDRx |= (1 << PinNo);
```

Syntax Explanation

- **DDRx**: Data Direction Register for the specified port.
    - DDRx controls each pin's direction on the port.
- **1 << PinNo**: Bit-shift operation that moves 1 to the bit position for the target pin (PinNo).
    - 1 << PinNo shifts the binary 1 by PinNo positions, creating a bitmask that targets only the specified pin.
- **|=**: Bitwise OR assignment operator that updates DDRx, setting the specified bit to 1 without affecting other bits in the register.

Simple Code Example

```
DDRB |= (1 << PB0);  // Set PB0 as output
```

Code Example Explanation

1. Accesses DDRB for Port B.
2. Uses (1 << PB0) to create a bitmask targeting only PB0.
3. Sets PB0 as an output without changing other pins in Port B.

Notes

- To reset the pin to input mode, use DDRx &= ~(1 << PinNo);.

Warnings

- Ensure that connected components can handle output signals.

---

4. Set Individual Pin as Input
What is Set Individual Pin as Input

Configuring an individual pin as input enables only that pin to read external signals, ideal for switches or sensors.

Use Purpose

- **Selective Input Configuration**: Configures only the specified pin as input.
- **Efficient Resource Use**: Avoids affecting other pins in the port.
- **Useful for Switches**: Reads the state of specific switches or sensors.

Syntax

```
DDRx &= ~(1 << PinNo);
```

Syntax Explanation

- **DDRx**: Data Direction Register for the specified port.
- **~(1 << PinNo)**: Bitwise NOT operation on (1 << PinNo) to create a bitmask with all bits set to 1 except the target pin.
- **&=**: Bitwise AND assignment operator clears the specific bit in DDRx, setting the targeted pin as input without affecting other bits.

Simple Code Example

```
DDRB &= ~(1 << PB1);   // Set PB1 as input
```

Code Example Explanation
1. Accesses DDRB.
2. Creates a bitmask to clear only the PB1 bit.
3. Sets PB1 to input mode, leaving other pins unchanged.

Notes
- Enable a pull-up resistor on the input pin if necessary.

Warnings
- Floating inputs can cause unreliable readings; use pull-up resistors if needed.

---

5. Set Pin Output High
What is Set Pin Output High

Setting a pin output high drives the pin to a logic level of 1, typically outputting a voltage (e.g., 5V or 3.3V), which can activate connected components like LEDs.

Use Purpose
- **Turn On Connected Devices**: Used to power LEDs, relays, etc.
- **Send High Logic Level**: Drives the connected pin to a high state.

Syntax
```
PORTx |= (1 << PinNo);
```

Syntax Explanation
- **PORTx**: Output register for the specified port.
- **1 << PinNo**: Left-shifts 1 by PinNo positions, creating a bitmask targeting the specific pin.
- **|=**: Bitwise OR operator that sets the targeted pin to high without affecting other pins.

Simple Code Example
```
PORTB |= (1 << PB0);  // Set PB0 high
```

Code Example Explanation

1. Accesses PORTB, the output register for Port B.
2. Sets only PB0 to a high state, turning on connected devices like LEDs.

Notes

- This command only works for pins previously set as outputs.

Warnings

- Directly driving high-power devices may damage the pin.

---

6. Set Pin Output Low

What is Set Pin Output Low

Setting a pin output low drives it to a logic level of 0 (ground), which can turn off connected components.

Use Purpose

- **Turn Off Connected Devices**: Turns off LEDs, relays, etc.
- **Send Low Logic Level**: Sets the connected pin to a low state.

Syntax

```
PORTx &= ~(1 << PinNo);
```

Syntax Explanation

- **PORTx**: Output register for the specified port.
- **~(1 << PinNo)**: Inverts the bitmask to set only the target pin low.
- **&=**: Bitwise AND operator that sets the targeted pin low without affecting other pins.

Simple Code Example

```
PORTB &= ~(1 << PB0);   // Set PB0 low
```

Code Example Explanation

1. Accesses PORTB, the output register for Port B.
2. Sets only PB0 to low, turning off any connected devices.

Notes

- Ensure the device connected can be controlled by a low signal.

Warnings

- Ensure proper grounding to avoid unexpected behavior.

---

7. Toggle Pin Output

What is Toggle Pin Output

Toggling a pin output switches its state between high and low. This is useful for creating blinking patterns in LEDs or generating clock signals.

Use Purpose

- **Create Blinking Effects**: Toggle LEDs on and off to create blinking lights.
- **Generate Clock Signals**: Toggle signals for clock pulses in communication protocols.
- **Switch Between States**: Useful in applications where an alternating signal is needed.

Syntax

```
PORTx ^= (1 << PinNo);
```

Syntax Explanation

- **PORTx**: Output register for the specified port.
- **1 << PinNo**: Left-shifts 1 by PinNo positions to create a bitmask that targets the specific pin.
- **^=**: Bitwise XOR operator that flips the state of the targeted pin, turning it from high to low or low to high.

Simple Code Example

```
PORTB ^= (1 << PB0);  // Toggle PB0
```

Code Example Explanation

1. Accesses PORTB, the output register for Port B.
2. Toggles PB0, flipping its current state.

Notes

- Toggle is useful for blinking effects and is often paired with a delay function to create visible on/off cycles.

Warnings

- Rapid toggling without delays may not be visible, especially with LEDs.

---

8. Read Individual Pin Input

What is Read Individual Pin Input

Reading a pin input checks its current state (high or low) without affecting its configuration. This is commonly used to detect the state of switches or sensors.

Use Purpose

- **Read External Signals**: Check if a switch is pressed or a sensor is activated.
- **Control Based on Input**: Respond to the state of an external device.
- **Simple Signal Detection**: Detects logic high (1) or low (0) on a pin.

Syntax

```
int val = (PINx & (1 << PinNo));
```

Syntax Explanation

- **PINx**: Input register for the specified port.
- **1 << PinNo**: Left-shifts 1 by PinNo positions, creating a bitmask targeting the desired pin.
- **&**: Bitwise AND checks if the target pin is high or low without changing other bits.
- **val**: The variable that stores the result of the read operation.

Simple Code Example

```
int button = (PINB & (1 << PB1));   // Read PB1 input
```

Code Example Explanation

1. Accesses PINB, the input register for Port B.
2. Reads PB1, storing its state in button.

Notes

- Ensure the pin is configured as input before reading to avoid errors.

Relevant Project Section

Project Name

Digital LED Control with Switch Input

Project Goal

To control an LED based on the state of a switch, demonstrating digital I/O functionality using AVR microcontroller pins.

Requirement Component

- AVR Microcontroller (e.g., ATmega328P)
- LED
- Push-button switch
- 330-ohm resistor (for LED)
- 10k-ohm resistor (for pull-up on the switch)

Component Connection Table

Component	Microcontroller Pin	Additional Notes
LED	PB0	330-ohm resistor in series
Switch	PB1	10k-ohm pull-up resistor

Connection Analysis
- **LED on PB0**: Lights up when PB0 is set to high, controlled by the switch state.
- **Switch on PB1**: Configured as input, with a pull-up resistor for stable readings.

Program Software Setup
1. Open Atmel Studio and create a new project.
2. Select the correct microcontroller model (e.g., ATmega328P).
3. Access and configure I/O registers:
     - Set PB0 as output for LED control.
     - Set PB1 as input for switch detection.
4. Enable the internal pull-up resistor on PB1.
5. Write the program code, as shown below.

Project Code

```c
#include <avr/io.h>

int main(void) {
    // Configure PB0 as output for LED
    DDRB |= (1 << PB0);
    // Configure PB1 as input for the switch
    DDRB &= ~(1 << PB1);
    // Enable internal pull-up resistor on PB1
    PORTB |= (1 << PB1);
    while (1) {
        // Check if the switch is pressed (PB1 reads low)
        if (!(PINB & (1 << PB1))) {
            PORTB |= (1 << PB0);  // Turn on LED
        } else {
            PORTB &= ~(1 << PB0); // Turn off LED
        }
    }
}
```

Save and Run
1. Save the code in Atmel Studio.
2. Compile and upload it to the AVR microcontroller using a programmer.
3. Test by pressing the switch and observing the LED behavior.

Check Output
- **When the switch is pressed**: PB1 reads low, and the LED on PB0 lights up.
- **When the switch is released**: PB1 reads high, and the LED turns off.

Chapter-5 Analog I/O

Chapter Overview

Analog I/O (Input/Output) enables AVR microcontrollers to interface with a wide range of real-world signals, including varying voltages from sensors, potentiometers, or even audio signals. Unlike digital I/O, which only detects or outputs binary signals (high or low), analog I/O lets the microcontroller handle continuous signals. This chapter will cover configuring and using analog inputs with an Analog-to-Digital Converter (ADC) and creating analog-like outputs using Pulse Width Modulation (PWM) on an AVR microcontroller using C in Atmel Studio.

Chapter Goal

- Understand the distinction between digital and analog signals and how the microcontroller processes them.
- Learn to use the ADC module to convert analog signals into digital values for processing.
- Implement PWM to generate analog-like outputs from digital pins.
- Complete a practical project that adjusts LED brightness using a potentiometer.

Rules

- **Analog Inputs**: Use the ADC to read continuous voltage signals.
- **Analog Outputs**: Use PWM to create analog-like signals from digital pins.
- **Bit Resolution**: Recognize that ADC resolution defines the precision of analog-to-digital conversions (usually 10-bit).
- **Reference Voltage**: Choose an appropriate reference voltage for scaling input signals.

Brief Introduction to ADC and PWM

Explanation of ADC Voltage Calculation

An ADC (Analog-to-Digital Converter) converts an analog input voltage into a digital value. To calculate the corresponding voltage for a given ADC digital value, we use this formula:

$$Voltage = \left(\frac{ADC\ Value}{Max\ ADC\ Value}\right) \times Reference\ Voltage$$

Let's break this formula into components to understand better:

What is an ADC?

- An ADC samples an analog signal (voltage) and converts it into a digital number.
- The range of values the ADC can output depends on its resolution, which is defined by the number of bits it uses.

Example ADC Resolution Calculation

For a 10-bit ADC

The resolution of an ADC is determined by the formula:

$$2^n = \{Number\ of\ Levels\}$$

Where:
- n=Number of bits of the ADC

For a 10-bit ADC, the resolution is 2^10 = 1024 levels (values from 0 to 1023).

This means the ADC has 1024 possible levels, ranging from 0 to 1023.

For a 12-bit ADC

For a **12-bit ADC**, the resolution is:

$$2^n = \{Number\ of\ Levels\}$$

For a 12-bit ADC, the resolution is 2^12 = 4096 levels (values from 0 to 4096).

Understanding the Formula

(a) Normalized Value

The normalized value is calculated as:

$$\frac{\text{ADC Value}}{\text{Max ADC Value}}$$

This part gives the **proportion of the reference voltage** represented by the ADC value.

For example:
- If the ADC Value is 512 (halfway in a 10-bit range), this fraction would be

$$\frac{512}{1024} \approx 0.5$$

This means the ADC value represents 50% of the reference voltage.

Reference Voltage

- The reference voltage defines the **maximum voltage** the ADC can measure.
- If the reference voltage is 3.3V, the ADC will map:
  - 0to 0V
  - 1023 (or Max ADC Value) to 3.3

(c) Multiply by Reference Voltage

- Multiplying the normalized value by the reference voltage converts the proportion into the actual voltage.

Step-by-Step Example
Imagine a system with:

- A **10-bit ADC** (Max ADC Value = 102310231023)
- A **Reference Voltage** of 5.0V5.0V5.0V
- A raw ADC reading of **256**

Step 1: Normalize the ADC Value

$$\frac{ADC\,Value}{Max\,ADC\,Value} = \frac{256}{1024} \approx 0.25$$

Step 2: Multiply by the Reference Voltage

Voltage=0.25×5.0=1.25V

So, an ADC value of 256 corresponds to 1.25V.

Visualisation

- ADC Resolution: 10-bit
- Reference Voltage: 3.3V

ADC Value	Proportion (ADCValue/1023)	Voltage (V)
0	0/1023=0.0	0.0V
256	256/1023≈0.25	0.25×3.3=0.825V
512	512/1023≈0.5	0.5×3.3=1.65V
768	768/1023≈0.75	0.75×3.3=2.475V
1023	1023/1023=1.0	1.0×3.3=3.3V

Syntax Table

Serial No	Topic	Syntax	Simple Example
1	Configure ADC	ADMUX	= (1 << REFS0);

2	Enable ADC	ADCSRA	= (1 << ADEN);
3	Start ADC Conversion	ADCSRA	= (1 << ADSC);
4	Read ADC Result	`int value = ADC;`	`int value = ADC;`
5	Configure PWM	TCCR0A	= (1 << COM0A1)
6	Set PWM Duty Cycle	`OCR0A = dutyCycle;`	`OCR0A = 128;`

Topic Explanations

Configure ADC
What is Configure ADC
Before starting analog-to-digital conversions, the ADC must be configured, which involves selecting the reference voltage and the ADC input channel.

Use Purpose
- **Set Reference Voltage**: Defines the maximum analog voltage the ADC can read, providing scaling for input signals.
- **Configure Input Channel**: Chooses the specific pin that will read the analog signal.

Syntax

```
ADMUX |= (1 << REFS0);
```

Syntax Explanation
ADMUX: The ADC Multiplexer Selection Register is used to configure various ADC settings.
- **(1 << REFS0)**: Sets the ADC reference voltage.

- Setting REFS0 to 1 chooses AVcc (typically 5V) as the reference voltage, setting this as the upper limit for the ADC readings.
- This reference voltage scales the conversion so that 5V corresponds to the maximum ADC value (1023 for a 10-bit ADC).

Simple Code Example

```
ADMUX |= (1 << REFS0);  // Set reference voltage to AVcc
```

Code Example Explanation
- Accesses the **ADMUX** register to configure the ADC.
- Sets the **REFS0** bit, configuring the ADC to interpret AVcc (usually 5V) as the highest possible input voltage.

Notes
- The reference voltage affects the resolution of analog readings; changing it requires modifying **ADMUX**.
- For applications requiring high precision, ensure a stable reference voltage.

Warnings
- Applying a voltage higher than the reference can damage the ADC or lead to inaccurate readings.

Enable ADC
What is Enable ADC
The ADC module must be enabled to perform conversions. Without enabling, the ADC hardware will not operate.

Use Purpose
- **Activate ADC Hardware**: Prepares the ADC for analog-to-digital conversions.

Syntax

```
ADCSRA |= (1 << ADEN);
```

1. **Syntax Explanation**
   o **ADCSRA**: The ADC Control and Status Register A, which manages ADC settings.
     ▪ **(1 << ADEN)**: Sets the **ADEN** bit (ADC Enable), which powers up and initializes the ADC for use.

Simple Code Example

```
ADCSRA |= (1 << ADEN);  // Enable the ADC
```

Code Example Explanation
- Accesses **ADCSRA**, the control register for ADC operations.
- Sets the **ADEN** bit, turning on the ADC module and enabling analog-to-digital functionality.

Notes
- The ADC must be enabled before initiating conversions.

Warnings
- Disabling the ADC during operation will halt any ongoing conversions, possibly leading to incorrect readings.

Start ADC Conversion
What is Start ADC Conversion
This command initiates an ADC conversion, converting the analog signal on the configured pin into a digital value.

Use Purpose
- **Begin Reading Analog Input**: Starts the ADC conversion process on the selected channel.

Syntax

```
ADCSRA |= (1 << ADSC);
```

Syntax Explanation
   o **ADCSRA**: The ADC Control and Status Register A.
     ▪ **(1 << ADSC)**: Sets the **ADSC** (ADC Start Conversion) bit to 1.

- When set, this bit initiates an analog-to-digital conversion on the configured input.
- The **ADSC** bit stays high while the conversion is in progress and clears automatically when the conversion completes.

Simple Code Example

```
ADCSRA |= (1 << ADSC);  // Start ADC conversion
```

Code Example Explanation
- Accesses **ADCSRA** to control the ADC.
- Starts a new ADC conversion by setting the **ADSC** bit.
- The program should monitor **ADSC** to confirm that the conversion has completed.

Notes
- Conversions are usually initiated manually unless the ADC is configured to run continuously.

Warnings
- Ensure the conversion completes before reading the result; otherwise, it may yield inaccurate values.

Read ADC Result
What is Read ADC Result
The ADC result register holds the digital value corresponding to the analog input. This value typically ranges from 0 to 1023 for a 10-bit ADC.

Use Purpose
- **Retrieve Analog Input Value**: Provides a digital representation of the analog input.

Syntax

```
int value = ADC;
```

2. **Syntax Explanation**
    ○ **ADC**: The combined 10-bit ADC result register.
        ■ This register combines **ADCL** (low byte) and **ADCH** (high byte) into a 10-bit digital value.
        ■ The value in this register represents the analog input scaled to a range of 0-1023.

Simple Code Example

```
int value = ADC;   // Read the ADC result
```

Code Example Explanation
- Reads the ADC register.
- Stores the digital equivalent of the analog input in the `value` variable.

Notes
- The result should be read only after confirming the conversion has completed.

Warnings
- Reading the result before the conversion is complete may yield incorrect data.

Configure PWM
What is Configure PWM
Configuring PWM allows the microcontroller to output an analog-like signal by adjusting the duty cycle of a digital output.
Use Purpose
- **Generate Analog-Like Signal**: Enables control of devices that respond to varying power levels, like LEDs and motors.

Syntax

```
TCCR0A |= (1 << COM0A1) | (1 << WGM00);
```

3. **Syntax Explanation**
    ○ **TCCR0A**: Timer/Counter Control Register for Timer 0, configuring the PWM output settings.

- **(1 << COM0A1)**: Configures PWM output to operate in non-inverting mode, where the output is high when counting up to the compare value.
- **(1 << WGM00)**: Enables Fast PWM mode, allowing PWM generation with the timer.

Simple Code Example

```
TCCR0A |= (1 << COM0A1) | (1 << WGM00);   // Configure PWM
```

Code Example Explanation
- Accesses **TCCR0A** to set up Timer 0 in Fast PWM mode.
- Configures the PWM output in non-inverted mode.

Notes
- Different PWM modes can affect frequency and duty cycle control.

Warnings
- Ensure the PWM mode matches the application requirements.

Set PWM Duty Cycle
What is Set PWM Duty Cycle
Adjusts the duty cycle of the PWM signal, controlling the average output power.

Use Purpose
- **Adjust Analog-Like Output**: Modifies the output voltage level for applications like dimming LEDs or controlling motor speed.

Syntax

```
OCR0A = dutyCycle;
```

Syntax Explanation
- **OCR0A**: Output Compare Register for Timer 0, used to control the PWM duty cycle.

- Setting this register changes the percentage of time the signal remains high.
- Duty cycle ranges from 0 (0% high) to 255 (100% high), where intermediate values simulate varying voltage levels.

Simple Code Example

```
OCR0A = 128;  // Set 50% duty cycle
```

Code Example Explanation
- Sets the **OCR0A** register to control the PWM output.
- A value of 128 creates a 50% duty cycle, generating an average voltage that is half of the supply voltage.

Notes
- Duty cycle adjustments provide smooth control over output power.

Warnings
- High duty cycles may produce excessive heat in connected devices.

Relevant Project Section

Project Name
Analog LED Brightness Control

Project Goal
To control LED brightness based on the voltage from a potentiometer, demonstrating analog-to-digital conversion and PWM output.

Requirement Component
- AVR Microcontroller (e.g., ATmega328P)
- LED
- Potentiometer
- 330-ohm resistor (for LED)

Component Connection Table

Component	Microcontroller Pin	Additional Notes
Potentiometer	ADC0	Connect to ADC0 for analog input
LED	OC0A (e.g., PB0)	Connected to PWM output

Connection Analysis

- **Potentiometer on ADC0**: Rotating the potentiometer varies the input voltage, which the ADC converts to a digital value.
- **LED on OC0A**: The PWM output, controlled by the potentiometer value, adjusts LED brightness.

Program Software Setup

1. Open Atmel Studio and create a new project.
2. Select the appropriate microcontroller model (e.g., ATmega328P).
3. Configure ADC and PWM registers:
   - Set ADC reference and channel for potentiometer input.
   - Configure PWM output for LED brightness control.
4. Write and upload the following program.

Project Code

```
#include <avr/io.h>
void ADC_init() {
    ADMUX |= (1 << REFS0);      // Set reference voltage to AVcc
    ADCSRA |= (1 << ADEN);      // Enable ADC
}

uint16_t ADC_read() {
    ADCSRA |= (1 << ADSC);         // Start conversion
    while (ADCSRA & (1 << ADSC));  // Wait for conversion to complete
    return ADC;                    // Return ADC result
}
void PWM_init() {
    TCCR0A |= (1 << COM0A1) | (1 << WGM00);  // Set non-inverting mode,
Fast PWM
    TCCR0B |= (1 << CS01);                    // Set prescaler to 8
```

```
    DDRB |= (1 << PB0);                    // Set PB0 as output
}

int main() {
    ADC_init();
    PWM_init();
    while (1) {
        uint16_t adc_value = ADC_read();    // Read potentiometer
value
        OCR0A = adc_value / 4;              // Map to 0-255 for PWM
    }
}
```

Save and Run

1. Save and compile the code in Atmel Studio.
2. Upload to the microcontroller using a programmer.
3. Adjust the potentiometer to observe LED brightness changes.

Check Output

- **Rotating the potentiometer**: Changes the LED brightness, achieving maximum brightness at full rotation and dimming as it rotates back.

Chapter-6 Advanced I/O

Chapter Overview

Advanced I/O operations allow AVR microcontrollers to handle more complex tasks, like responding to external events without continuous polling and generating precise time-based outputs. This chapter covers interrupt-based I/O, external interrupts, and advanced timer functionalities using C in Atmel Studio. By the end, you'll understand how to set up interrupts, handle external events, and use timers for precise control.

Chapter Goal

- Learn to configure and use external interrupts for responsive I/O.
- Understand how timers and counters work in AVR microcontrollers.
- Implement advanced I/O techniques to create time-dependent or event-driven responses.
- Complete a project using an external interrupt to control an LED with a button press.

Rules

- **Interrupts**: Use interrupts to trigger functions without polling.
- **External Interrupts**: Detect changes on specific pins to respond immediately.
- **Timers and Counters**: Set up timers to generate precise intervals or event-based actions.
- **Debouncing**: Account for switch bounce to avoid false triggers on external interrupts.

Brief Introduction to Interrupts and Timers

- **Interrupts**: Interrupts are signals that tell the microcontroller to pause its current task and run a specific function. Interrupt-based I/O improves responsiveness and efficiency by avoiding the need for continuous polling.

- **External Interrupts**: An external interrupt is triggered by a change (e.g., rising or falling edge) on a specific pin, allowing the microcontroller to react immediately to external events, like a button press.
- **Timers and Counters**: Timers allow precise time-based operations by counting microcontroller clock cycles. They are often used for PWM generation, event timing, and frequency measurement.

Syntax Table

Serial No	Topic	Syntax	Simple Example
1	Enable Global Interrupts	sei();	sei();
2	Configure External Interrupt	EICRA	= (1 << ISC01);
3	Enable External Interrupt	EIMSK	= (1 << INT0);
4	Set Up Timer in CTC Mode	TCCR1B	= (1 << WGM12);
5	Set Timer Compare Value	OCR1A = value;	OCR1A = 15624;
6	Enable Timer Interrupt	TIMSK1	= (1 << OCIE1A);

Topic Explanations

Enable Global Interrupts
What is Enable Global Interrupts
Enabling global interrupts allows the microcontroller to respond to any interrupt request. Without this, interrupts are ignored even if configured.

Use Purpose

- ○ **Activate All Interrupts**: Ensures that the microcontroller is ready to respond to any interrupt events.
- ○ **Necessary Step for Interrupts**: Required to make all interrupt configurations effective.

Syntax

```
sei();
```

Syntax Explanation

- ○ **sei()**: A built-in function that sets the global interrupt enable bit in the microcontroller's status register, allowing all configured interrupts to trigger.

Simple Code Example

```
sei();  // Enable global interrupts
```

Code Example Explanation

- Calls **sei()** to enable all interrupts across the microcontroller.
- Ensures that any configured interrupt can now be triggered.

Notes

- Place this function after configuring interrupts to activate them.

Warnings

- Failing to enable global interrupts will prevent any interrupts from occurring.

Configure External Interrupt
What is Configure External Interrupt

Configures an external interrupt on a specific pin, triggered by a change on that pin, such as a rising edge (low to high transition) or falling edge (high to low transition).

Use Purpose

- **Detect External Events**: Allows the microcontroller to respond instantly to external signals like button presses.
- **Control Trigger Condition**: Configure the type of change (rising, falling, or both edges) that triggers the interrupt.

Syntax

```
EICRA |= (1 << ISC01);
```

Syntax Explanation

- **EICRA**: External Interrupt Control Register, which determines the trigger condition.
- **(1 << ISC01)**: Sets the ISC01 bit to trigger on a falling edge. Other configurations allow triggering on a rising edge or on any change.

Simple Code Example

```
EICRA |= (1 << ISC01);  // Set external interrupt on falling edge
```

Code Example Explanation

- Accesses **EICRA** to set the trigger condition.
- Configures an external interrupt to activate on a falling edge.

Notes

- Different bits in **EICRA** allow various trigger conditions; consult the datasheet for additional options.

Warnings

- Ensure the trigger condition matches the desired input event to avoid unintended interrupts.

Enable External Interrupt
What is Enable External Interrupt

Enables the configured external interrupt on a specific pin, allowing the microcontroller to respond to changes on that pin.

Use Purpose

- **Activate Configured Interrupt**: Ensures the configured external interrupt is active.
- **Prepare for External Signals**: Allows the microcontroller to monitor the designated pin for external changes.

Syntax

```
EIMSK |= (1 << INT0);
```

Syntax Explanation

- **EIMSK**: External Interrupt Mask Register, used to enable specific external interrupts.
- **(1 << INT0)**: Sets the INT0 bit to enable the external interrupt on INT0 (usually associated with a specific pin).

Simple Code Example

```
EIMSK |= (1 << INT0);  // Enable external interrupt 0
```

Code Example Explanation

- Accesses **EIMSK** to enable the external interrupt.
- Activates interrupt 0, allowing it to respond to the previously configured trigger.
  Notes
- **EIMSK** has multiple bits, one for each external interrupt channel (e.g., INT0, INT1).
  Warnings
- Disabling an interrupt channel during operation may lead to missed signals.

Set Up Timer in CTC Mode
What is Set Up Timer in CTC Mode

Configuring a timer in CTC (Clear Timer on Compare Match) mode allows it to count up to a specified value, generating an interrupt or toggling an output when it reaches this value.

Use Purpose

- **Create Precise Timing Events**: CTC mode is useful for generating fixed intervals.
- **Generate Periodic Outputs**: Set up regular time-based actions like blinking LEDs or creating frequency signals.

Syntax

```
TCCR1B |= (1 << WGM12);
```

Syntax Explanation

- **TCCR1B**: Timer/Counter Control Register B for Timer 1.
- **(1 << WGM12)**: Sets the WGM12 bit to enable CTC mode, where the timer resets to zero after reaching the compare match value.

Simple Code Example

```
TCCR1B |= (1 << WGM12);  // Set Timer 1 to CTC mode
```

Code Example Explanation

- Accesses **TCCR1B** to configure the timer.
- Sets **WGM12** to enable CTC mode, preparing the timer for fixed-interval operations.

Notes

- CTC mode is commonly used for creating timed interrupts and frequency generation.

Warnings

- Incorrectly setting timer mode bits may lead to unexpected behaviors.

Set Timer Compare Value
What is Set Timer Compare Value

Defines the timer's target value for CTC mode. When the timer reaches this value, it resets and can trigger an interrupt or toggle an output.

Use Purpose

- **Specify Timing Duration**: Controls the interval length for periodic actions.
- **Trigger Interrupts at Set Intervals**: Enables time-based actions without continuous polling.

Syntax

```
OCR1A = value;
```

Syntax Explanation

- **OCR1A**: Output Compare Register for Timer 1, channel A.
  - Setting a value in **OCR1A** defines the timer's target count, determining the interval duration.

Simple Code Example

```
OCR1A = 15624;  // Set timer compare value for 1-second interval at 1
MHz with prescaler
```

Code Example Explanation

- Assigns 15624 to **OCR1A**, setting the timer to reset after reaching this count.
- Triggers an interrupt when the timer reaches the compare value.

Notes

- Calculate the compare value based on the microcontroller's clock speed and the desired interval.

Warnings

- Incorrect compare values may lead to incorrect timing or missed interrupts.

Enable Timer Interrupt

What is Enable Timer Interrupt

Enables an interrupt for a timer's compare match, allowing it to trigger an ISR when the timer reaches the compare value.

Use Purpose
- **Automate Time-Based Events**: Allows the timer to automatically trigger code execution at set intervals.
- **Control Event Frequency**: Set up precise recurring events, such as toggling an LED or reading sensors.

Syntax

```
TIMSK1 |= (1 << OCIE1A);
```

Syntax Explanation
- **TIMSK1**: Timer Interrupt Mask Register for Timer 1, which enables timer interrupts.
- **(1 << OCIE1A)**: Sets the OCIE1A bit to enable the compare match interrupt on channel A.

Simple Code Example

```
TIMSK1 |= (1 << OCIE1A);  // Enable Timer 1 compare match interrupt
```

Code Example Explanation
- Accesses **TIMSK1** to enable the timer interrupt.
- Activates the compare match interrupt for Timer 1, channel A.

Notes
- Use this in combination with **sei()** to ensure the interrupt is recognized.

Warnings
- Failing to enable the interrupt mask bit will prevent the timer interrupt from executing.

Relevant Project Section

Project Name
External Interrupt Button-Controlled LED with Timer

Project Goal
To control an LED using an external button interrupt and set up a timer-based blink pattern, demonstrating both interrupt-driven input and time-based output.

Requirement Component

- AVR Microcontroller (e.g., ATmega328P)
- LED
- Push-button switch
- 330-ohm resistor (for LED)
- 10k-ohm pull-up resistor (for the button)

Component Connection Table

Component	Microcontroller Pin	Additional Notes
LED	PB0	LED connected with a resistor to ground
Button	INT0 (e.g., PD2)	External interrupt pin, pull-up resistor required

Connection Analysis
- **Button on INT0**: The button press triggers an external interrupt, controlling the LED.
- **LED on PB0**: LED responds to the timer interrupt, creating a controlled blink pattern.

Program Software Setup
1. Open Atmel Studio and create a new project.
2. Select the correct microcontroller model (e.g., ATmega328P).
3. Configure external interrupts for the button and set up Timer 1 in CTC mode for LED blinking.
4. Write and upload the following code.

Project Code

```c
#include <avr/io.h>
#include <avr/interrupt.h>

void setup_interrupt() {
    EICRA |= (1 << ISC01);      // Set INT0 to trigger on falling edge
    EIMSK |= (1 << INT0);       // Enable external interrupt INT0
}

void setup_timer() {
    TCCR1B |= (1 << WGM12);     // Set Timer 1 to CTC mode
    OCR1A = 15624;              // Set compare value for 1Hz blink at 1
MHz with prescaler 64
    TIMSK1 |= (1 << OCIE1A);    // Enable Timer 1 compare match
interrupt
    TCCR1B |= (1 << CS12) | (1 << CS10); // Set prescaler to 1024 and
start timer
}

ISR(INT0_vect) {
    PORTB ^= (1 << PB0);        // Toggle LED state
}

ISR(TIMER1_COMPA_vect) {
    PORTB ^= (1 << PB0);        // Blink LED
}

int main() {
    DDRB |= (1 << PB0);         // Set PB0 as output for LED
    PORTD |= (1 << PD2);        // Enable pull-up resistor on PD2 for
button

    setup_interrupt();
    setup_timer();
    sei();                      // Enable global interrupts

    while (1) {
        // Main loop does nothing, waiting for interrupts
    }
}
```

Save and Run
1. Save and compile the code in Atmel Studio.
2. Upload it to the AVR microcontroller using a programmer.
3. Press the button to toggle the LED's blinking pattern.

Check Output
- **Pressing the button**: Toggles the LED state, which blinks
  according to the timer interrupt.

Chapter-7 Variables and Constants

Chapter Overview

Variables and constants are fundamental components in programming. Variables hold data that can change as a program executes, while constants are fixed values that remain unchanged throughout. This chapter will cover how to declare, initialize, modify, and use variables and constants in C for AVR microcontrollers, with a focus on efficient memory use and code readability.

Chapter Goal

- Understand the difference between variables and constants.
- Learn how to declare, initialize, and use variables effectively.
- Understand when to use constants and how they improve code stability.
- Complete a practical project to demonstrate the use of variables and constants.

Rules

- **Data Types**: Every variable must be declared with a data type (e.g., `int`, `float`, `char`).
- **Scope**: Variables can have local (function-specific) or global (accessible throughout the program) scope.
- **Constants**: Declared with `const` or `#define`, constants maintain a fixed value and enhance code readability and reliability.
- **Naming Conventions**: Use meaningful names for variables and uppercase letters for constants.

Brief Introduction to Variables and Constants

- **Variables**: Memory locations with assigned names where data can be stored, modified, and retrieved. Variable values can change during program execution.
- **Constants**: Fixed values assigned to names in memory that remain unchanged. Constants provide stable values for

parameters that should not change, such as the maximum buffer size or mathematical constants.

Syntax Table

Serial No	Topic	Syntax	Simple Example
1	Variable Declaration	`type variableName;`	`int counter;`
2	Variable Initialization	`type variableName = value;`	`float voltage = 5.0;`
3	Declare Multiple Variables	`type var1, var2;`	`int x, y;`
4	Constant Declaration	`const type constName = value;`	`const int MAX = 10;`
5	Constant Using #define	`#define CONST_NAME value`	`#define PI 3.14159`
6	Modify Variable Value	`variableName = newValue;`	`counter = 10;`

Topic Explanations
Variable Declaration
What is Variable Declaration
Declaring a variable creates a named storage location in memory and specifies the data type of the value it will store. Declaring a variable reserves memory space so that the program can store and retrieve values dynamically.

Use Purpose
- **Store and Manage Data**: Store numbers, characters, or other data types.
- **Temporary Storage**: Use variables to store data that may change as the program runs, such as sensor readings or calculations.

Syntax

```
type variableName;
```

Syntax Explanation
- **type**: Specifies the data type of the variable, such as int (integer), float (floating-point number), or char (character).
- **variableName**: The unique identifier or name of the variable, following C naming rules. Names should start with a letter or underscore and cannot contain spaces or special characters (except underscores).

Simple Code Example

```
int counter;   // Declares an integer variable named counter
```

Code Example Explanation
- The code creates an integer variable named counter.
- counter can store any integer value, and the value can change throughout the program.

Notes
- Variables should have descriptive names to make the code easier to understand.
- Declaring variables at the beginning of the function or program helps with readability.

Variable Initialization
What is Variable Initialization
Initialization assigns an initial value to a variable at the time of declaration. Initializing variables helps avoid undefined behavior by ensuring the variable starts with a known value.
Use Purpose
- **Assign Initial Value**: Prepare the variable for immediate use, eliminating unpredictable data.
- **Set Starting Value for Calculations**: Establish a baseline or starting point for calculations or logic.

Syntax

```
type variableName = value;
```

Syntax Explanation
- **type**: Specifies the data type of the variable.
- **variableName**: The name of the variable.
- **value**: The initial value assigned to the variable. The type of the value must match the variable type (e.g., assigning an integer value to an int variable).

Simple Code Example

```
float voltage = 5.0;  // Initializes voltage with a value of 5.0
```

Code Example Explanation
- Declares a float variable named voltage.
- Assigns an initial value of 5.0 to voltage.
Notes
- Initialization improves code reliability by ensuring variables hold a defined value from the start.
- It's common practice to initialize variables, especially counters or accumulators, to zero.
Warnings
- Using a variable before initialization can lead to unpredictable or incorrect behavior.

Declare Multiple Variables
What is Declare Multiple Variables

Declaring multiple variables of the same type in one line allows for efficient code that groups related variables together.

Use Purpose

- **Concise Declaration**: Reduces redundancy by grouping similar variables in a single line.
- **Improves Readability**: Declares related variables together, making the code cleaner and more organized.

Syntax

```
type var1, var2;
```

Syntax Explanation

- **type**: Specifies the data type of both variables.
- **var1, var2**: Names of the variables, separated by a comma. Each variable can be used individually within the program.

Simple Code Example

```
int x, y;  // Declares two integer variables x and y
```

Code Example Explanation

- Declares two integer variables, x and y.
- Both x and y can be assigned values independently and used in calculations.

Notes

- Use meaningful names to clarify each variable's purpose.

Warnings

- Declaring too many variables in one line may decrease readability.

Constant Declaration
What is Constant Declaration

Declaring a constant creates a named value that cannot be modified. Constants are especially useful for values that remain the same, such as configuration settings or mathematical values.

Use Purpose
- **Define Fixed Values**: Sets a constant value that remains unchanged, enhancing code stability.
- **Improves Code Readability**: Provides a descriptive name to a fixed value, making the code easier to understand.

Syntax

```
const type constName = value;
```

Syntax Explanation
- **const**: Keyword that makes the variable read-only.
- **type**: Data type of the constant, such as int or float.
- **constName**: The name of the constant, typically in uppercase to distinguish it from variables.
- **value**: The fixed value assigned to the constant.

Simple Code Example

```
const int MAX = 10;   // Defines a constant MAX with a value of 10
```

Code Example Explanation
- Declares a constant MAX with type int.
- Sets MAX to 10, a value that cannot be modified later in the program.

Notes
- Constants enhance program stability by preventing accidental changes to critical values.

Warnings
- Attempting to modify a constant will result in a compiler error.

Constant Using #define
What is Constant Using #define
#define is a preprocessor directive that replaces all occurrences of a constant name with a specific value during compilation. #define constants do not use memory space.

Use Purpose
- **Memory Efficiency**: #define constants do not occupy memory.
- **Global Value**: Can be used throughout the program for consistent value references.

Syntax

```
#define CONST_NAME value
```

Syntax Explanation
- **#define**: Directive used to define a constant at compile-time.
- **CONST_NAME**: Typically uppercase to indicate a constant.
- **value**: The fixed value assigned to the constant. The compiler substitutes every instance of CONST_NAME with this value.

Simple Code Example

```
#define PI 3.14159   // Defines PI as 3.14159
```

Code Example Explanation
- Defines PI with a value of 3.14159.
- Every occurrence of PI in the code will be replaced by 3.14159 at compile time.

Notes
- **#define** is useful for defining constants that must be accessible across multiple files.

Warnings
- No type checking is done with #define constants, so use carefully.

Modify Variable Value
What is Modify Variable Value
Modifying a variable allows you to change its value based on program requirements. This is essential for storing intermediate results or updating values in response to program logic.

Use Purpose
- **Update Data Dynamically**: Allows changing data as conditions change within the program.
- **Perform Calculations**: Enables storing intermediate results or updated values for later use.

Syntax

```
variableName = newValue;
```

Syntax Explanation
- **variableName**: The name of the variable whose value you wish to change.
- **newValue**: The new value to assign, which must match the variable's data type.

Simple Code Example

```
counter = 10;  // Assigns a new value of 10 to counter
```

Code Example Explanation
- Modifies counter, assigning it a new value of 10.
- Changes to counter will reflect throughout the program.

Notes
- Updating variables is critical in loops and conditionals for tracking state changes.

Warnings
- Ensure the new value is of the correct data type.

Relevant Project Section
Project Name
Temperature Conversion (Celsius to Fahrenheit)
Project Goal
To create a simple program that converts temperature from Celsius to Fahrenheit using variables for input and output values, with constants for the conversion factors.

Requirement Component
- AVR Microcontroller (e.g., ATmega328P)
- Serial communication for displaying the output (optional)

Component Connection Table

Component	Microcontroller Pin	Additional Notes
Serial Interface	TX, RX (optional)	For displaying results

Connection Analysis
This project uses only variables and constants for calculations. It's designed to reinforce the concept of variables and constants without requiring external components.

Program Software Setup

1. Open Atmel Studio and create a new project.
2. Configure the microcontroller for basic input/output.

Project Code

```c
#include <avr/io.h>
#include <stdio.h>
#define CONVERT_FACTOR 1.8    // Conversion factor for Celsius to
Fahrenheit
#define OFFSET 32             // Offset for Fahrenheit calculation
int main() {
    float celsius = 25.0;    // Variable to store temperature in Celsius
    float fahrenheit;        // Variable to store temperature in
Fahrenheit

    // Perform the conversion
    fahrenheit = (celsius * CONVERT_FACTOR) + OFFSET;

    // Optional: Print the result to a serial monitor
    printf("Temperature in Fahrenheit: %.2f\n", fahrenheit);

    while(1);
}
```

Save and Run
1. Save and compile the code in Atmel Studio.
2. Run the program to see the result (if using a serial monitor).

Check Output
- The output should display the converted temperature in Fahrenheit.

Chapter-8 Data Types

Chapter Overview
Data types in C define the kind of data a variable can hold, as well as the memory space it occupies. Selecting the correct data type is crucial in microcontroller programming to optimize memory usage and ensure accurate calculations. This chapter covers the fundamental data types available in C for AVR microcontrollers, including integers, floating-point numbers, and special types like char and bool, with practical examples.

Chapter Goal

- Understand different data types available in C and their memory requirements.
- Learn when to use each data type effectively.
- Practice declaring and using data types in AVR programming.
- Complete a project to apply different data types in an LED control application.

Rules

- **Size and Range**: Choose data types that fit the expected data range to optimize memory use.
- **Signed vs. Unsigned**: Decide between signed and unsigned based on whether negative values are required.
- **Use Descriptive Names**: Choose meaningful variable names to enhance readability.
- **Floating Point Precision**: Be mindful of floating-point precision when using float and double.

Brief Introduction to Data Types
Data types are categorizations of data that tell the compiler how much memory to allocate and how to interpret the bit pattern in memory. C offers various data types, including integers, floating-point numbers, characters, and Boolean values, each with specific purposes.

Syntax Table

Serial No	Topic	Syntax	Simple Example
1	Integer	`int variableName;`	`int count;`
2	Unsigned Integer	`unsigned int variableName;`	`unsigned int items;`
3	Character	`char variableName;`	`char letter;`
4	Boolean	`bool variableName;`	`bool isOn;`
5	Floating Point	`float variableName;`	`float voltage;`
6	Double Precision	`double variableName;`	`double temperature;`

Topic Explanations

Integer
What is Integer
An integer is a data type used to store whole numbers (no decimal point). Integers are one of the most commonly used data types, as they represent counts, IDs, and other values without fractions.
Use Purpose
- **Store Whole Numbers**: Used for counters, loop variables, and indexes.
- **Memory Efficiency**: Uses less memory compared to floating-point types, which is beneficial for microcontrollers with limited memory.

Syntax

```
int variableName;
```

Syntax Explanation

- **int**: Data type keyword for integer.
- **variableName**: Name of the integer variable. Should follow naming conventions (no spaces or special characters).

Simple Code Example

```
int count = 10;  // Declares an integer variable named count and
initializes it to 10
```

Code Example Explanation

- Declares an integer variable named `count`.
- Initializes `count` with the value 10, which can change as the program executes.

Notes

- **Range**: The range of `int` is typically from -32768 to 32767 for 16-bit systems, though it may vary with system architecture.
- AVR microcontrollers often have limited memory, so choose data types that fit your application's needs.

Warnings

- Using values outside the range will cause an overflow or underflow.

Unsigned Integer
What is Unsigned Integer
An unsigned integer is similar to a regular integer but can only store non-negative values. By excluding negative values, unsigned integers can store larger positive values within the same memory space.

Use Purpose

- **Non-negative Counts**: Suitable for storing values that cannot be negative, like array indexes, counts, and sizes.
- **Extended Range**: Doubles the positive range compared to signed integers.

Syntax

```
unsigned int variableName;
```

Syntax Explanation

- **unsigned int**: Keyword indicating an integer that only stores positive values.
- **variableName**: Name of the unsigned integer variable.

Simple Code Example

```
unsigned int items = 20;   // Declares an unsigned integer named items
and initializes it to 20
```

Code Example Explanation

- Declares an unsigned integer variable named items.
- Sets the initial value of items to 20, which can be incremented or decremented but will not store negative values.

Notes

- **Range**: For a 16-bit unsigned integer, the range is 0 to 65535.

Warnings

- Attempting to assign a negative value will result in a compilation error or incorrect behavior.

Character
What is Character

The char data type stores a single character, such as a letter, symbol, or digit. Characters are stored as integers using ASCII encoding, where each character has a unique numeric value.

Use Purpose

- **Store Text or Symbols**: Used to represent letters, punctuation, or other symbols.
- **Data for Communication**: Commonly used in serial communication to send and receive characters.

Syntax

```
char variableName;
```

Syntax Explanation

- **char**: Keyword representing a character.
- **variableName**: Name of the character variable.

Simple Code Example

```
char letter = 'A';  // Declares a character variable named letter and
initializes it with 'A'
```

Code Example Explanation

- Declares a character variable named `letter`.
- Initializes `letter` with the character A.

Notes

- Characters are stored as 8-bit integers (0-255) using ASCII encoding.
- Characters can be treated as numbers in operations.

Warnings

- Declaring a `char` variable without initializing may yield unexpected results.

Boolean
What is Boolean

A Boolean data type, often declared as `bool`, stores a binary value of either true or false. AVR-GCC defines `true` as 1 and `false` as 0.

Use Purpose

- ○ **Flag Values**: Used as flags to control program flow or indicate states.
- ○ **Condition Testing**: Simplifies conditional statements (e.g., while loops).

Syntax

```
bool variableName;
```

Syntax Explanation

- **bool**: Data type representing Boolean values.
- **variableName**: Name of the Boolean variable.

Simple Code Example

```
bool isOn = true;  // Declares a Boolean variable named isOn and
initializes it to true
```

Code Example Explanation

- Declares a Boolean variable named isOn.
- Sets the initial value of isOn to true.

Notes

- The Boolean type requires the <stdbool.h> library in C.

Warnings

- Using values other than 0 and 1 may lead to unexpected behavior.

Floating Point
What is Floating Point

The float data type stores decimal numbers, representing both integer and fractional values. Floating-point numbers are useful for calculations requiring precision.

Use Purpose

- **Decimal Values**: Used for measurements like voltage, temperature, or speed.
- **Mathematical Operations**: Essential for calculations requiring precision beyond integers.

Syntax

```
float variableName;
```

Syntax Explanation
- **float**: Keyword representing a floating-point number.
- **variableName**: Name of the floating-point variable.

Simple Code Example

```
float voltage = 3.3;  // Declares a float variable named voltage and
initializes it with 3.3
```

Code Example Explanation
- Declares a `float` variable named `voltage`.
- Sets the initial value of `voltage` to 3.3, which can represent decimal values.

Notes
- The precision of a `float` is typically up to six decimal places.
- Floating-point operations are slower and use more memory than integers.

Warnings
- Be mindful of precision limitations when performing calculations.

Double Precision
What is Double Precision
The `double` data type provides higher precision for floating-point numbers compared to `float`, but at the cost of additional memory usage.

Use Purpose
- **Increased Precision**: Useful when more accuracy is needed for calculations.
- **Scientific Calculations**: Ideal for complex formulas or where slight inaccuracies are unacceptable.

Syntax

```
double variableName;
```

Syntax Explanation

- **double**: Keyword representing a double-precision floating-point number.
- **variableName**: Name of the double-precision variable.

Simple Code Example

```
double temperature = 98.6;  // Declares a double variable named
temperature and initializes it with 98.6
```

Code Example Explanation

- Declares a `double` variable named `temperature`.
- Initializes `temperature` with 98.6, allowing for more precision in calculations.

Notes

- `double` has a precision of about 15 decimal places on most systems.
- Double-precision numbers require more processing time and memory.

Warnings

- Consider memory limitations on microcontrollers when using `double`.

Relevant Project Section

Project Name
LED Brightness and Mode Control

Project Goal
To control an LED's brightness and mode using different data types to manage brightness levels, states, and mode flags.

Requirement Component

- AVR Microcontroller (e.g., ATmega328P)
- LED
- Push-button
- Resistor (330-ohm for LED)

Component Connection Table

Component	Microcontroller Pin	Additional Notes
LED	PB0	Connected to ground via resistor
Push-button	PD2 (INT0)	Connected for mode toggle

Connection Analysis

- **LED**: Controlled via PWM duty cycle to adjust brightness.
- **Push-button**: Used to toggle between brightness modes.

Program Software Setup

1. Open Atmel Studio and create a new project.
2. Set up PWM for LED brightness control and configure an interrupt for the push-button.

Project Code

```
#include <avr/io.h>
#include <stdbool.h>

#define MAX_BRIGHTNESS 255

void PWM_init() {
    // Set non-inverting mode for PWM
    TCCR0A |= (1 << COM0A1) | (1 << WGM00) | (1 << WGM01);
    TCCR0B |= (1 << CS01);       // Set prescaler to 8
    DDRB |= (1 << PB0);          // Set PB0 as output
}

int main() {
    uint8_t brightness = 128;    // Variable for LED brightness
```

```
    bool mode = false;              // Boolean to toggle between brightness
modes

    PWM_init();

    while (1) {
        if (mode) {
            brightness = MAX_BRIGHTNESS;    // Full brightness
        } else {
            brightness = brightness / 2;    // Half brightness
        }

        OCR0A = brightness;    // Update PWM duty cycle for LED
    }
}
```

Save and Run

1. Save and compile the code in Atmel Studio.
2. Adjust brightness by changing the value of brightness.

Check Output

- **Mode 1**: Sets LED to full brightness.
- **Mode 2**: Dims LED to half brightness.

Chapter-9 Data Type Conversion

Chapter Overview

Data type conversion is essential in programming, especially in embedded systems where memory and performance are critical. In AVR microcontroller programming, we often need to convert between data types, like converting integer values to floating-point for precise calculations or changing data types to fit specific functions. This chapter will cover both implicit and explicit conversions, including integer-to-float conversions, integer-to-string conversions, and working with mixed data types.

Chapter Goal

- Understand the difference between implicit and explicit data type conversions.
- Learn how to perform conversions between integers, floats, and strings.
- Practice using conversions in arithmetic and display functions.
- Complete a practical project that demonstrates data type conversions for an ADC sensor reading displayed as a string.

Rules

- **Implicit Conversions**: Automatic conversions done by the compiler, often from smaller to larger data types.
- **Explicit Conversions (Casting)**: Conversions specified by the programmer to ensure data is treated in a particular way.
- **Overflow/Underflow**: Converting from a larger to a smaller type may cause overflow if the value exceeds the range.
- **Loss of Precision**: Converting floating-point numbers to integers may lose fractional parts.

Brief Introduction to Data Type Conversion

Data type conversion, also known as type casting, changes a variable from one data type to another. Conversions are necessary when working with different types in calculations, passing arguments to functions, or displaying data. C supports two types of conversions:

- **Implicit Conversion**: The compiler automatically changes a variable's type if needed.
- **Explicit Conversion (Casting)**: The programmer specifies the conversion to ensure precise control over how the data is interpreted.

Syntax Table

Serial No	Topic	Syntax	Simple Example
1	Integer to Float Conversion	`float var = (float)intValue;`	`float result = (float)sum;`
2	Float to Integer Conversion	`int var = (int)floatValue;`	`int count = (int)price;`
3	Integer to String Conversion	`sprintf(str, "%d", intValue);`	`sprintf(buffer, "%d", num);`
4	Float to String Conversion	`sprintf(str, "%.2f", floatValue);`	`sprintf(buffer, "%.2f", voltage);`
5	String to Integer Conversion	`int num = atoi(str);`	`int result = atoi(input);`
6	String to Float Conversion	`float num = atof(str);`	`float result = atof(value);`

Topic Explanations

Integer to Float Conversion
What is Integer to Float Conversion
Converting an integer to a float allows for more precise arithmetic operations by adding decimal points. This conversion is helpful in AVR applications where you need fractional results from integer values, such as when scaling sensor values.

Use Purpose
- o **Improve Precision**: Allows calculations that need decimal values.
- o **Mixed-Type Arithmetic**: Ensures accurate results when integers and floats are combined.

Syntax

```
float var = (float)intValue;
```

Syntax Explanation
- **(float)**: Explicitly casts the integer intValue to a floating-point type.
- **var**: The variable that will hold the converted float value.

Simple Code Example

```
int sum = 25;
float result = (float)sum;   // Converts sum to 25.0 as a float
```

Code Example Explanation
- Declares an integer sum and assigns it a value of 25.
- Casts sum to float and stores it in result as 25.0.

Notes
- Converting to float adds a decimal, allowing calculations with higher precision.

Warnings
- Casting large integers to float may lose precision due to float limitations.

Float to Integer Conversion

What is Float to Integer Conversion

Converting a float to an integer removes the decimal part, effectively rounding down the value. This conversion is useful when an integer is needed for indexing, counting, or storing sensor data without fractional values.

Use Purpose

- **Integer-Based Logic**: Simplifies control structures or indexing by removing decimal points.
- **Memory Efficiency**: Saves space by converting from 4-byte float to 2-byte integer on AVR.

Syntax

```
int var = (int)floatValue;
```

Syntax Explanation

- **(int)**: Explicitly casts the floatValue to an integer.
- **var**: Holds the converted integer value.

Simple Code Example

```
float price = 19.99;
int roundedPrice = (int)price;   // Converts price to 19
```

Code Example Explanation

- Declares a float price with a value of 19.99.
- Casts price to an integer, which removes the decimal, resulting in 19.

Notes

- This conversion drops the decimal part, effectively rounding down the number.

Warnings

- Precision is lost when converting floats to integers, as decimal data is truncated.

Integer to String Conversion
What is Integer to String Conversion
Converting an integer to a string is common in applications involving display output, such as showing numerical values on an LCD. C's `sprintf()` function is often used for this purpose.

Use Purpose
- **Display Output**: Used when numbers must be displayed as text.
- **Format Control**: Enables flexible formatting of integer data for display.

Syntax

```
sprintf(str, "%d", intValue);
```

Syntax Explanation
- **sprintf()**: A standard library function to format data as a string.
- **str**: The destination character array where the result will be stored.
- **%d**: Format specifier for integer values.

Simple Code Example

```
int num = 42;
char buffer[10];
sprintf(buffer, "%d", num);   // Converts num to string "42" in buffer
```

Code Example Explanation
- Declares an integer num with a value of 42.
- Uses `sprintf()` to convert num to a string, storing "42" in `buffer`.

Notes
- Make sure `buffer` is large enough to hold the string.

Warnings
- Overflow may occur if the integer is too large for the allocated buffer.

Float to String Conversion
What is Float to String Conversion
Converting a float to a string is necessary for displaying or transmitting numerical values with decimal points. The `sprintf()` function allows format specifiers to control decimal precision.
Use Purpose
- **Display Precision**: Used when decimal precision is needed in display output.
- **Formatted Output**: Enables controlling the number of decimal places shown.

Syntax

```
sprintf(str, "%.2f", floatValue);
```

Syntax Explanation
- **str**: Destination string to store the formatted float.
- **%.2f**: Format specifier that formats the float with two decimal places.

Simple Code Example

```
float voltage = 3.14159;
char buffer[10];
sprintf(buffer, "%.2f", voltage);  // Converts voltage to "3.14"
```

Code Example Explanation
- Converts `voltage` to a string with two decimal places (3.14).
- Stores the string "3.14" in `buffer`.
Notes
- Adjust the format specifier (e.g., `%.2f`, `%.3f`) to control decimal places.
Warnings
- Ensure buffer size is sufficient to hold the resulting string.

String to Integer Conversion
What is String to Integer Conversion
Converting a string to an integer allows numerical data stored as text to be used in calculations or comparisons. `atoi()` is commonly used for this in C.

Use Purpose
- **User Input Parsing**: Allows conversion of text input into numerical values.
- **Text-Based Data Handling**: Parses text data into integers for arithmetic.

Syntax

```
int num = atoi(str);
```

Syntax Explanation
- **atoi()**: Function to convert a string to an integer.
- **str**: The string to be converted.

Simple Code Example

```
char input[] = "123";
int number = atoi(input);   // Converts "123" to integer 123
```

Code Example Explanation
- Converts the string "123" to the integer 123.

Notes
- Ensure the string represents a valid integer to avoid undefined behavior.

Warnings
- `atoi()` does not check for invalid input, so ensure the string contains only numeric characters.

String to Float Conversion

What is String to Float Conversion

atof() converts a string representation of a decimal number to a floating-point value, enabling text-based decimal data to be used in calculations.

Use Purpose

- **User Input Parsing**: Converts decimal string input to float for calculations.
- **Data Processing**: Used in applications that parse decimal data from text.

Syntax

```
float num = atof(str);
```

Syntax Explanation

- **atof()**: Function to convert a string to a float.
- **str**: The string to convert.

Simple Code Example

```
char value[] = "3.14";
float result = atof(value);   // Converts "3.14" to float 3.14
```

Code Example Explanation

- Converts the string "3.14" to the floating-point number 3.14.

Notes

- atof() is useful for converting string data to floating-point for calculations.

Warnings

- atof() does not check for invalid input, so ensure the string format is valid.

Relevant Project Section

Project Name
Sensor Data Display with Data Conversion

Project Goal
To read a sensor value via ADC, convert it from integer to float for scaling, then display the formatted result as a string on an LCD or serial output.

Requirement Component

- AVR Microcontroller (e.g., ATmega328P)
- Potentiometer (to simulate an analog sensor)
- LCD Display (optional) or Serial Monitor

Component Connection Table

Component	Microcontroller Pin	Additional Notes
Potentiometer	ADC0 (Analog Pin)	Analog input
LCD/Serial Display	TX (Serial)	Optional for output display

Connection Analysis

- **Potentiometer**: Connected to ADC to simulate sensor data.
- **LCD/Serial Display**: Used to display formatted sensor data as a string.

Program Software Setup

1. Open Atmel Studio and create a new project.
2. Set up ADC for reading potentiometer values and configure serial communication.

Project Code

```c
#include <avr/io.h>
#include <stdio.h>
#include <stdlib.h>

#define MAX_VOLTAGE 5.0

void ADC_init() {
    ADMUX |= (1 << REFS0);      // Set reference voltage to AVcc
    ADCSRA |= (1 << ADEN);      // Enable ADC
}

uint16_t ADC_read() {
    ADCSRA |= (1 << ADSC);        // Start conversion
    while (ADCSRA & (1 << ADSC)); // Wait for conversion to complete
    return ADC;
}

int main() {
    char buffer[10];
    uint16_t adcValue;
    float voltage;

    ADC_init();

    while (1) {
        adcValue = ADC_read();
        voltage = (float)adcValue * MAX_VOLTAGE / 1023.0;   // Convert
ADC to voltage
        sprintf(buffer, "%.2f V", voltage);   // Convert voltage to
string

        // Optional: Display buffer content via serial or LCD

    }
}
```

Save and Run

1. Save and compile the code in Atmel Studio.
2. Run the code, displaying the voltage reading as a string.

Check Output

- **LCD/Serial Display**: Shows formatted sensor data in voltage (e.g., "2.45 V").

Chapter-10 Control Structures

Chapter Overview

Control structures are fundamental in programming and enable you to control the flow of execution based on conditions and repetitions. In AVR microcontroller programming, control structures are used to handle decisions, loop through actions, and create responses based on external inputs. This chapter covers decision-making structures (if, else, switch) and loops (for, while, do-while) to help you develop efficient, structured code for AVR applications.

Chapter Goal

- Understand different types of control structures in C.
- Learn how to implement decision-making and loops effectively.
- Use control structures to manage program flow and respond to sensor inputs.
- Complete a project that demonstrates the use of control structures to control LED states based on sensor values.

Rules

- **Conditional Statements**: Use if/else and switch to execute code based on conditions.
- **Looping**: Use loops (for, while, do-while) to repeat code until a condition is met or a set number of times.
- **Avoid Infinite Loops**: Ensure there is a condition to exit loops to prevent locking up the microcontroller.
- **Use Clear Logic**: Write control structures with clear, meaningful conditions to make the code easy to understand and maintain.

Brief Introduction to Control Structures

Control structures are blocks of code that dictate how and when other parts of the code are executed. They are categorized into:

- **Conditional Statements**: Execute code only if certain conditions are met.
- **Loops**: Repeatedly execute code until a condition is no longer met.

Syntax Table

Serial No	Topic	Syntax	Simple Example
1	If Statement	`if (condition) { /* code */ }`	`if (sensor > 50) { LED_ON(); }`
2	If-Else Statement	`if (condition) { /* code */ } else { /* code */ }`	`if (temp > 30) { FAN_ON(); } else { FAN_OFF(); }`
3	Switch Statement	`switch (variable) { case value: /* code */ }`	`switch (mode) { case 1: LED_ON(); break; }`
4	For Loop	`for (init; condition; increment) { /* code */ }`	`for (i = 0; i < 5; i++) { LED_ON(); }`
5	While Loop	`while (condition) { /* code */ }`	`while (button == 1) { LED_TOGGLE(); }`
6	Do-While Loop	`do { /* code */ } while (condition);`	`do { LED_ON(); } while (sensor < 20);`

Topic Explanations
If Statement
What is If Statement

The `if` statement evaluates a condition and executes the code inside its block if the condition is true. This structure is useful for decision-making based on inputs or program states.

Use Purpose

- **Decision Making**: Execute code only when specific conditions are met.
- **Conditional Execution**: Control program flow based on real-time data (e.g., sensor values).

Syntax

```
if (condition) {
    // Code to execute if condition is true
}
```

Syntax Explanation

- **if**: The keyword that initiates a conditional statement.
- **condition**: The condition to evaluate. If true, the code block will execute; if false, it will skip.

Simple Code Example

```
int sensor = 60;
if (sensor > 50) {
    LED_ON();
}
```

Code Example Explanation

- Checks if the `sensor` value is greater than 50.
- If true, it calls the `LED_ON()` function.

Notes

- Conditions in C return `true` for any non-zero value and `false` for zero.

Warnings

- Ensure the condition is well-defined to prevent unintended code execution.

If-Else Statement

What is If-Else Statement

The `if-else` structure provides an alternative action if the `if` condition is false. This is useful when there are two possible outcomes, such as turning a fan on if the temperature is high or off if it is low.

Use Purpose

- **Two-Way Decision**: Executes one block of code if the condition is true and another if false.
- **Control States**: Handles mutually exclusive actions.

Syntax

```
if (condition) {
    // Code if true
} else {
    // Code if false
}
```

Syntax Explanation

- **else**: The keyword that specifies the alternative code block if the `if` condition is false.

Simple Code Example

```
int temp = 35;
if (temp > 30) {
    FAN_ON();
} else {
    FAN_OFF();
}
```

Code Example Explanation

- o Checks if `temp` is above 30.
- o Turns the fan on if true; otherwise, it turns it off.

Notes

- o You can chain multiple `if-else` conditions to handle complex decisions.

Warnings

- o Ensure the `else` block represents the correct alternative action.

Switch Statement
What is Switch Statement

The `switch` statement executes different blocks of code based on the value of a variable. It is helpful when there are multiple specific conditions to check, such as various modes or states.

Use Purpose

- o **Multi-Way Decision Making**: Simplifies complex `if-else` chains.
- o **Organized Code Flow**: Makes code cleaner and more readable for multiple specific values.

Syntax

```
switch (variable) {
    case value1:
        // Code for value1
        break;
    case value2:
        // Code for value2
        break;
    default:
        // Code if no cases match
}
```

Syntax Explanation

- **switch**: Keyword that starts the multi-way decision structure.
- **case value**: Each case compares the variable to a specific value.
- **break**: Ends each case block to prevent fall-through.

Simple Code Example

```
int mode = 2;
switch (mode) {
    case 1:
        LED_ON();
        break;
    case 2:
        LED_OFF();
        break;
    default:
        LED_TOGGLE();
}
```

Code Example Explanation

- Checks the value of mode.
- Turns the LED on for mode 1, off for mode 2, and toggles otherwise.

Notes

- **default** is optional but recommended to handle unexpected values.

Warnings

- Omitting break may lead to fall-through, where multiple cases execute.

For Loop
What is For Loop

The for loop repeats a block of code a set number of times, useful for tasks like iterating through arrays or repeating actions a specific number of times.

Use Purpose

- o **Fixed Iterations**: Execute code a predetermined number of times.
- o **Controlled Repetition**: Set up initialization, condition, and increment in one line.

Syntax

```
for (initialization; condition; increment) {
    // Code to execute
}
```

Syntax Explanation

- o **initialization**: Sets the loop counter's initial value.
- o **condition**: Evaluates before each loop iteration; if false, the loop ends.
- o **increment**: Updates the loop counter after each iteration.

Simple Code Example

```
for (int i = 0; i < 5; i++) {
    LED_TOGGLE();
}
```

Code Example Explanation

- o Toggles the LED five times.
- o i starts at 0, increments after each loop, and stops after reaching 5.

Notes

- o The loop will exit once the condition becomes false.

Warnings

- o Avoid off-by-one errors by carefully setting the loop's conditions.

While Loop
What is While Loop

A while loop repeats a block of code as long as a condition is true. It is useful when the number of repetitions is unknown but depends on a condition.

Use Purpose

- o **Condition-Based Looping**: Repeats code based on real-time conditions.
- o **Event-Driven Execution**: Commonly used in polling or waiting for events.

Syntax

```
while (condition) {
    // Code to execute
}
```

Syntax Explanation

- o **condition**: The loop condition, checked before each iteration. The loop executes as long as it remains true.

Simple Code Example

```
while (button == 1) {
    LED_TOGGLE();
}
```

Code Example Explanation

- o Toggles the LED repeatedly while button is pressed.

Notes

- o The loop exits as soon as the condition becomes false.

Do-While Loop
What is Do-While Loop

A `do-while` loop executes the code block once, then repeats it while the condition is true. It guarantees that the code runs at least once.

Use Purpose

- **Guaranteed Execution**: Useful when the code should run at least once regardless of the condition.
- **Condition-Dependent Repetition**: Checks the condition after executing the code.

Syntax

```
do {
    // Code to execute
} while (condition);
```

Syntax Explanation

- **do**: Starts the loop and executes the code block once.
- **while**: Checks the condition at the end of each iteration.

Simple Code Example

```
int sensor = 15;
do {
    LED_ON();
} while (sensor < 20);
```

Code Example Explanation

- Turns on the LED at least once.
- The loop repeats until `sensor` reaches 20 or more.

Notes

- The `do-while` loop always runs the code block at least once.

Relevant Project Section

Project Name
LED Control Based on Temperature Reading

Project Goal
To read temperature data and control an LED based on preset
temperature levels using control structures.

Requirement Component

- AVR Microcontroller (e.g., ATmega328P)
- Temperature Sensor (e.g., LM35)
- LED
- Resistor (330-ohm for LED)

Component Connection Table

Component	Microcontroller Pin	Additional Notes
Temperature Sensor	ADC0	Analog input
LED	PB0	Connect through resistor

Connection Analysis

- **Temperature Sensor**: Connected to ADC0 for reading
  analog temperature data.
- **LED**: The LED state changes based on temperature levels
  using control structures.

Program Software Setup

1. Open Atmel Studio and create a new project.
2. Set up ADC for temperature readings.

Project Code

```c
#include <avr/io.h>

void ADC_init() {
    ADMUX |= (1 << REFS0);      // Set reference voltage to AVcc
    ADCSRA |= (1 << ADEN);      // Enable ADC
}

uint16_t ADC_read() {
    ADCSRA |= (1 << ADSC);        // Start conversion
    while (ADCSRA & (1 << ADSC)); // Wait for conversion to complete
    return ADC;
}

int main() {
    DDRB |= (1 << PB0);         // Set PB0 as output for LED
    uint16_t temperature;

    ADC_init();

    while (1) {
        temperature = ADC_read(); // Read temperature sensor

        if (temperature > 500) {
            PORTB |= (1 << PB0);   // Turn on LED if temperature is high
        } else {
            PORTB &= ~(1 << PB0); // Turn off LED if temperature is low
        }
    }
}
```

Save and Run

1. Save and compile the code in Atmel Studio.
2. Run the program and observe the LED response based on temperature input.

Check Output

- **High Temperature**: LED turns on.
- **Low Temperature**: LED turns off.

Chapter-11 Arithmetic Operators

Chapter Overview

Arithmetic operators are essential in programming, enabling basic mathematical calculations like addition, subtraction, multiplication, and division. In AVR microcontroller programming, arithmetic operations are crucial for tasks like sensor data processing, timing calculations, and real-time adjustments based on input values. This chapter covers the main arithmetic operators in C, along with examples demonstrating their use in AVR applications.

Chapter Goal

- Understand the basic arithmetic operators in C.
- Learn how to apply arithmetic operators to perform calculations on microcontrollers.
- Use arithmetic operators in real-world AVR applications, such as controlling sensor data and adjusting output based on input.
- Complete a project to practice using arithmetic operators in a practical application.

Rules

- **Operator Precedence**: C follows operator precedence rules (e.g., multiplication before addition).
- **Data Type Compatibility**: Ensure that data types are compatible with operations to avoid overflow or truncation.
- **Division by Zero**: Avoid dividing by zero, as it causes undefined behavior.
- **Modulo on Negative Values**: Modulo operations with negative values may yield unexpected results depending on compiler behavior.

Brief Introduction to Arithmetic Operators

Arithmetic operators in C allow mathematical operations on numbers. In AVR microcontroller programming, these operators are used for tasks such as scaling sensor readings, calculating delays, and setting thresholds. The main arithmetic operators include:

- **Addition (+)**: Adds two values.
- **Subtraction (-)**: Subtracts one value from another.
- **Multiplication (*)**: Multiplies two values.
- **Division (/)**: Divides one value by another.
- **Modulo (%)**: Finds the remainder after division of one value by another.

Syntax Table

Serial No	Topic	Syntax	Simple Example
1	Addition	`result = a + b;`	`sum = num1 + num2;`
2	Subtraction	`result = a - b;`	`difference = value - offset;`
3	Multiplication	`result = a * b;`	`product = length * width;`
4	Division	`result = a / b;`	`average = total / count;`
5	Modulo	`result = a % b;`	`remainder = total % divisor;`

Topic Explanations

Addition
What is Addition

The addition operator (+) sums two values. In microcontroller programming, addition is commonly used to calculate totals, add offsets, and increase counts.

Use Purpose

- **Accumulate Values**: Useful for adding values over time, like sensor data.
- **Increase Counters**: Commonly used in loops and counters for tracking events.

Syntax

```
result = a + b;
```

Syntax Explanation

- **a** and **b**: Operands representing numbers to be added.
- **result**: Variable that stores the sum of a and b.

Simple Code Example

```
int num1 = 10;
int num2 = 20;
int sum = num1 + num2;  // sum is 30
```

Code Example Explanation

- Adds num1 and num2.
- Stores the result, 30, in sum.

Notes

- Ensure variable types are compatible to avoid overflow in case of large numbers.

Warnings

- Adding large integers may cause overflow if the result exceeds the variable's range.

Subtraction
What is Subtraction

The subtraction operator (-) calculates the difference between two values. It's useful for determining distances, reducing values, or adjusting data.

Use Purpose

- o **Decrease Counts**: Used in loops or counters.
- o **Calculate Differences**: Useful for setting thresholds and making comparisons.

Syntax

```
result = a - b;
```

Syntax Explanation

- o **a** and **b**: Operands representing numbers, with b subtracted from a.
- o **result**: Variable that stores the difference of a - b.

Simple Code Example

```
int value = 50;
int offset = 10;
int result = value - offset;   // result is 40
```

Code Example Explanation

- o Subtracts offset from value.
- o Stores the result, 40, in result.

Notes

- o Be mindful of underflow when subtracting large values from smaller ones.

Multiplication
What is Multiplication

The multiplication operator (*) calculates the product of two values. In AVR applications, multiplication is often used to scale values or calculate area, volume, or other products.

Use Purpose

- o **Scale Values**: Useful for adjusting sensor data or setting proportional values.
- o **Area/Volume Calculations**: For computing space or dimensions.

Syntax

```
result = a * b;
```

Syntax Explanation

- o **a** and **b**: Operands representing numbers to be multiplied.
- o **result**: Variable that stores the product of a and b.

Simple Code Example

```
int length = 5;
int width = 4;
int area = length * width;  // area is 20
```

Code Example Explanation

- o Multiplies length by width.
- o Stores the result, 20, in area.

Notes

- o Multiplying two integers results in an integer. If fractional results are needed, use float or double.

Division

What is Division

The division operator (/) divides one value by another. Division is common for calculating averages, rates, and scaled-down values.

Use Purpose

- **Calculate Ratios**: Useful for setting proportions or average values.
- **Scaling Down Values**: Reduces values for display or control purposes.

Syntax

```
result = a / b;
```

Syntax Explanation

- **a** and **b**: Operands where a is divided by b.
- **result**: Variable that stores the quotient of a / b.

Simple Code Example

```
int total = 100;
int count = 4;
int average = total / count;   // average is 25
```

Code Example Explanation

- Divides `total` by `count`.
- Stores the result, 25, in `average`.

Notes

- Division of integers discards any remainder. Use `float` or `double` for precise results.

Warnings

- Avoid dividing by zero, as it causes undefined behavior.

Modulo
What is Modulo

The modulo operator (%) returns the remainder after division. It's commonly used in AVR programming for tasks like timing, cycling through values, or determining if a number is even or odd.

Use Purpose

- **Cycle Through Values**: Useful in circular buffers or repeating patterns.
- **Determine Even/Odd**: Returns 0 for even numbers and 1 for odd.

Syntax

```
result = a % b;
```

Syntax Explanation

- **a** and **b**: Operands where a is divided by b, and the remainder is returned.
- **result**: Variable that stores the remainder of a % b.

Simple Code Example

```
int total = 10;
int divisor = 3;
int remainder = total % divisor;   // remainder is 1
```

Code Example Explanation

- Divides `total` by `divisor` and returns the remainder.
- Stores the result, 1, in `remainder`.

Notes

- The modulo operation is particularly useful in time-based applications for repeating cycles.

Warnings

- Avoid using modulo with zero as the divisor.

Relevant Project Section

Project Name
LED Blink Pattern Control

Project Goal
To control an LED blinking pattern based on arithmetic operations, such as adjusting brightness in a PWM cycle or changing blink rate based on sensor input.

Requirement Component

- AVR Microcontroller (e.g., ATmega328P)
- LED
- Push-button
- Resistor (330-ohm for LED)

Component Connection Table

Component	Microcontroller Pin	Additional Notes
LED	PB0	Connect through resistor
Button	PD2	Used for toggling blink speed

Connection Analysis

- **LED**: Controls brightness or blink rate using arithmetic operations.
- **Button**: Toggles between different blink rates for the LED.

Program Software Setup

1. Open Atmel Studio and create a new project.
2. Set up a timer for the LED blink rate and configure a button interrupt to toggle modes.

Project Code

```c
#include <avr/io.h>
#include <util/delay.h>

int main() {
    DDRB |= (1 << PB0);  // Set PB0 as output for LED
    int delay_time = 100; // Initial delay time in ms

    while (1) {
        PORTB ^= (1 << PB0);  // Toggle LED state
        _delay_ms(delay_time);  // Delay to control blink speed

        // Adjust delay time using arithmetic operators
        delay_time = (delay_time + 50) % 300;  // Cycle delay between
50 and 300 ms
    }
}
```

Save and Run

1. Save and compile the code in Atmel Studio.
2. Observe the LED blink pattern changing based on the arithmetic operation in `delay_time`.

Check Output

- **LED Blink Rate**: The LED blinks at a changing rate, cycling between different speeds as per the arithmetic calculation.

Chapter-12 Boolean Operators

Chapter Overview

Boolean operators are essential tools for making complex logical decisions in programming. In AVR microcontroller applications, Boolean operators are used to combine multiple conditions, such as checking multiple sensor inputs, controlling devices based on multiple thresholds, or managing states. This chapter covers the main Boolean operators in C and provides examples of their application in AVR programming.

Chapter Goal

- Understand the basic Boolean operators in C.
- Learn how to combine multiple conditions using Boolean operators.
- Use Boolean operators in real-world AVR applications, such as checking multiple sensor thresholds and executing actions based on combined conditions.
- Complete a project that demonstrates Boolean operators to control multiple LEDs based on sensor input conditions.

Rules

- **Operator Types**: C has three main Boolean operators: && (AND), || (OR), and ! (NOT).
- **Order of Operations**: Boolean operators follow specific precedence rules, with ! evaluated before &&, and && before ||. Use parentheses to clarify complex expressions.
- **Short-Circuit Evaluation**: In && and || expressions, evaluation stops as soon as the result is determined (e.g., false && anything is always false).
- **Binary Results**: Boolean operators evaluate to true (1) or false (0), and can be used in conditional statements, such as if and while.

Brief Introduction to Boolean Operators

Boolean operators allow combining multiple logical conditions in a single expression, making them crucial for complex decision-making. The three main Boolean operators are:

- **AND (&&)**: True if both conditions are true.
- **OR (||)**: True if at least one condition is true.
- **NOT (!)**: Inverts the truth value of a condition (true becomes false, and vice versa).

Syntax Table

Serial No	Topic	Syntax	Simple Example
1	AND (&&)	`condition1 && condition2`	`if (temp > 50 && speed < 100)`
2			
3	NOT (!)	`!condition`	`if (!isOn)`

Topic Explanations

1. **AND (&&)**
   What is AND (&&)
   The AND operator (&&) checks if both conditions are true. If both conditions are met, the entire expression evaluates to `true`; otherwise, it evaluates to `false`. This is useful when multiple conditions need to be satisfied before executing a block of code.
   Use Purpose
   - ○ **Combined Condition Checks**: Ensures that all conditions are met for a particular action.
   - ○ **Logical Control**: Commonly used for setting safety checks, such as verifying that multiple sensors are in a safe range.

Syntax

```
if (condition1 && condition2) {
    // Code to execute if both conditions are true
}
```

Syntax Explanation

- **condition1** and **condition2**: Logical expressions or variables being checked.
- **if (condition1 && condition2)**: Executes the code block only if both conditions are true.

Simple Code Example

```
int temp = 70;
int speed = 40;
if (temp > 50 && speed < 100) {
    FAN_ON();
}
```

Code Example Explanation

- Checks if temp is greater than 50 and speed is less than 100.
- If both conditions are true, it turns the fan on with FAN_ON().

Notes

- AND expressions are useful for ensuring multiple conditions are met simultaneously.

Warnings

- Be careful with complex expressions; use parentheses to clarify grouping of conditions.

OR (||)
What is OR (||)

The OR operator (||) checks if at least one of the conditions is true. If any one condition is met, the expression evaluates to true; otherwise, it evaluates to false. OR is useful when multiple acceptable conditions trigger the same action.

Use Purpose

- ○ **Alternative Condition Checks**: Allows multiple ways to trigger an action.
- ○ **Logical Flexibility**: Useful for checking if any one of multiple states is active.

Syntax

```
if (condition1 || condition2) {
    // Code to execute if either condition is true
}
```

Syntax Explanation

- **condition1** and **condition2**: Logical expressions or variables being checked.
- **if (condition1 || condition2)**: Executes the code block if either condition is true.

Simple Code Example

```
int sensor = 1;
int button = 0;
if (sensor == 1 || button == 1) {
    LED_ON();
}
```

Code Example Explanation

- Checks if sensor is equal to 1 or button is equal to 1.
- If either condition is true, it turns on the LED by calling LED_ON().

Notes

- OR expressions are useful when an action needs to be triggered by multiple possible conditions.

Warnings

- Be mindful of || and && precedence when combining multiple conditions.

NOT (!)

What is NOT (!)

The NOT operator (!) inverts the Boolean value of a condition. If the condition is `true`, ! makes it `false`, and vice versa. This operator is useful for conditions that require an action when something is false.

Use Purpose

- **Negate Conditions**: Check for the opposite state of a condition.
- **Simplify Expressions**: Reduces complex conditions by inverting a simpler one.

Syntax

```
if (!condition) {
    // Code to execute if condition is false
}
```

Syntax Explanation

- **condition**: Logical expression or variable being inverted.
- **if (!condition)**: Executes the code block if the condition is `false`.

Simple Code Example

```
int isOn = 0;
if (!isOn) {
    LED_OFF();
}
```

Code Example Explanation

- Checks if isOn is `false` (0).
- If isOn is `false`, it calls `LED_OFF()` to turn off the LED.

Notes

- NOT expressions are often used in cases where an action is needed when a state is off or inactive.

Warnings

- Use ! carefully in complex expressions to avoid unintended logic.

Relevant Project Section

Project Name
Dual Sensor-Based LED Control

Project Goal
To control an LED based on two sensor readings, using Boolean operators to determine when the LED should turn on or off based on combined conditions.

Requirement Component

- AVR Microcontroller (e.g., ATmega328P)
- Temperature Sensor (e.g., LM35)
- Light Sensor (e.g., LDR with ADC)
- LED
- Resistor (330-ohm for LED)

Component Connection Table

Component	Microcontroller Pin	Additional Notes
Temperature Sensor	ADC0	Analog input for temperature
Light Sensor	ADC1	Analog input for light level
LED	PB0	Connect through resistor

Connection Analysis

- **Temperature Sensor**: Reads analog temperature data.
- **Light Sensor**: Reads ambient light data.
- **LED**: Controlled based on temperature and light readings using Boolean operators.

Program Software Setup

1. Open Atmel Studio and create a new project.
2. Set up ADC for reading the temperature and light sensor data.

Project Code

```c
#include <avr/io.h>
void ADC_init() {
    ADMUX |= (1 << REFS0);       // Set reference voltage to AVcc
    ADCSRA |= (1 << ADEN);       // Enable ADC
}
uint16_t ADC_read(uint8_t channel) {
    ADMUX = (ADMUX & 0xF8) | (channel & 0x07);   // Select ADC channel
    ADCSRA |= (1 << ADSC);        // Start conversion
    while (ADCSRA & (1 << ADSC)); // Wait for conversion to complete
    return ADC;
}
int main() {
    DDRB |= (1 << PB0);           // Set PB0 as output for LED
    uint16_t temperature;
    uint16_t light;
    uint16_t temp_threshold = 512;  // Temperature threshold
    uint16_t light_threshold = 400; // Light level threshold
    ADC_init();
    while (1) {
        temperature = ADC_read(0);  // Read temperature sensor
        light = ADC_read(1);        // Read light sensor

        // Turn LED on if temperature exceeds threshold AND light is
below threshold
        if (temperature >= temp_threshold && light < light_threshold) {
            PORTB |= (1 << PB0);   // Turn on LED
        } else {
            PORTB &= ~(1 << PB0);  // Turn off LED
        }
    }
}
```

Save and Run

1. Save and compile the code in Atmel Studio.
2. Run the code, observing the LED behavior based on the temperature and light readings.

Check Output

- **High Temperature and Low Light**: LED turns on when both conditions are met.
- **Any Other Condition**: LED turns off if either condition is not met.

Chapter-13 Compound Operators

Chapter Overview

Compound operators combine an operation (e.g., addition, subtraction, bitwise) with assignment, allowing programmers to simplify and optimize code. In embedded systems, where memory and processing power are often limited, using compound operators can improve both performance and readability. This chapter explains each compound operator, with examples relevant to AVR microcontroller programming.

Chapter Goal

- Understand the purpose and function of each compound operator.
- Learn practical applications for each operator in embedded programming.
- Complete a hands-on project to apply compound operators in controlling microcontroller outputs.

Rules

- **Syntax Structure**: Each compound operator follows a op= b, combining an operation with assignment.
- **Compatible Data Types**: Works with integers, but some operators can be used with floats and chars.
- **Memory Efficiency**: Compound operators are concise, reducing code size.
- **Error Handling**: Proper use prevents overflow, underflow, and logical errors in bitwise operations.

Brief Introduction to Compound Operators

Compound operators in C allow you to combine arithmetic, logical, and bitwise operations with assignment in a single, concise expression. Instead of writing a = a + b, you can write a += b. These operators make code easier to read and more efficient, essential in resource-limited environments like microcontroller programming.

Syntax Table

Serial No	Topic	Syntax	Simple Example
1	Addition Assignment	`a += b;`	`counter += 5;`
2	Subtraction Assignment	`a -= b;`	`value -= 3;`
3	Multiplication Assignment	`a *= b;`	`scale *= 2;`
4	Division Assignment	`a /= b;`	`total /= 4;`
5	Modulus Assignment	`a %= b;`	`count %= 3;`
6	Bitwise AND Assignment	`a &= b;`	`flags &= 0x0F;`
7	Bitwise OR Assignment	`a`	`= b;`
8	Bitwise XOR Assignment	`a ^= b;`	`flags ^= 0xFF;`
9	Left Shift Assignment	`a <<= b;`	`value <<= 1;`
10	Right Shift Assignment	`a >>= b;`	`value >>= 2;`

Detailed Breakdown for Each Command

1. Addition Assignment (+=)

What is Addition Assignment

The += operator combines addition with assignment, adding a specified value to an existing variable and updating the variable with the new result. This operator is especially useful for incrementing counters and accumulators in loops or repetitive tasks.

Use Purpose

- **Loop Incrementation**: Increase values in loops.
- **Accumulators**: Calculate sums over multiple iterations.

Syntax

```
a += b;
```

Syntax Explanation

- **a**: The target variable that will store the result.
- **b**: The value to add to a.
- Result: a becomes a + b.

Simple Code Example

```
int counter = 0;
counter += 5;  // counter now equals 5
```

Code Example Explanation

- Initializes counter to 0.
- Adds 5 to counter and updates counter to hold the new value of 5.

Notes

The += operator is commonly used in for loops to increment counters.

2. Subtraction Assignment (-=)

What is Subtraction Assignment

The -= operator subtracts a specified value from a variable and stores the result back in that variable. Instead of writing a = a - b, a -= b reduces both code length and potential for errors in repetitive calculations.

Use Purpose

- **Loop Decrementing**: Decrease values in a loop.
- **Adjustments**: Reduce variable values by a set amount.

Syntax

```
a -= b;
```

Syntax Explanation

- **a**: Target variable for storing the result.
- **b**: Value to subtract from a.
- Result: a becomes a - b.

Simple Code Example

```
int value = 10;
value -= 3;  // value now equals 7
```

Code Example Explanation

- Sets value to 10.
- Subtracts 3 from value, resulting in 7.

Notes

Useful in countdowns, loop decrements, and adjusting values.

Warnings

Be cautious with unsigned types, as subtracting too much may result in wrap-around.

3. Multiplication Assignment (*=)

What is Multiplication Assignment

The *= operator multiplies a variable by a specified value and stores the result in that variable. This operator is useful for scaling values or performing repeated multiplications without writing a = a * b.

Use Purpose

- **Scaling**: Increase values by a multiplier.
- **Exponential Growth**: Apply growth or scaling in loops.

Syntax

```
a *= b;
```

Syntax Explanation

- **a**: Variable to store the result.
- **b**: Value to multiply with a.
- Result: a becomes a * b.

Simple Code Example

```
int scale = 2;
scale *= 4;  // scale now equals 8
```

Code Example Explanation

- Sets scale to 2.
- Multiplies scale by 4, updating it to 8.

Notes

Useful for multiplying values in loops or increasing by a fixed multiplier.

Warnings

Multiplying large values may cause overflow, especially in small data types.

4. Division Assignment (/ =)

What is Division Assignment

The /= operator divides a variable by a specified value and updates the variable with the quotient. Instead of writing a = a / b, you can write a /= b, reducing code length.

Use Purpose

- **Scaling Down**: Decrease values in loops.
- **Averages and Reductions**: Often used for reducing sums.

Syntax

```
a /= b;
```

Syntax Explanation

- **a**: Variable to store the result.
- **b**: Value by which a is divided.
- Result: a becomes a / b.

Simple Code Example

```
int total = 20;
total /= 4;   // total now equals 5
```

Code Example Explanation

- Initializes total to 20.
- Divides total by 4, updating it to 5.

Notes

Useful for scaling down or averaging data.

Warnings

Ensure b is not zero to prevent division errors.

5. Modulus Assignment (%=)

What is Modulus Assignment

The %= operator divides a variable by a specified value and assigns the remainder back to the variable. It's useful in cases where values need to cycle within a certain range, such as counters.

Use Purpose

- **Cycle Counting**: Keeps values within a range, like in cyclic counters.
- **Modulo Operations**: Used for indexing circular buffers or repetitive sequences.

Syntax

```
a %= b;
```

Syntax Explanation

- **a**: Variable to store the result.
- **b**: Value to divide a by.
- Result: a becomes the remainder of a / b.

Simple Code Example

```
int count = 10;
count %= 3;  // count now equals 1
```

Code Example Explanation

- Sets count to 10.
- Updates count to the remainder of 10 divided by 3, which is 1.

Notes

Commonly used in cycling or looping values within a range.

Warnings

Undefined behavior for division by zero.

6. Bitwise AND Assignment (&=)

What is Bitwise AND Assignment

The &= operator performs a bitwise AND operation between two values and stores the result in the left variable. This is commonly used to mask bits, effectively turning off specific bits in a register while keeping others unchanged.

Use Purpose

- **Masking Bits**: Clears specific bits while preserving others.
- **Flag Management**: Controls flags by clearing select bits.

Syntax

```
a &= b;
```

Syntax Explanation

- a and b are compared bit by bit.
- Each bit in a is set to 1 only if the corresponding bit in b is also 1.

Simple Code Example

```
int flags = 0b1010;    // binary: 1010
flags &= 0b1100;       // flags now equals 0b1000
```

7. Bitwise OR Assignment (| =)

What is Bitwise OR Assignment

The bitwise OR assignment operator (| =) performs a bitwise OR between two values and stores the result in the left variable. This operator is frequently used to set specific bits in a register without changing the values of other bits.

Use Purpose

- **Setting Bits**: Forces specific bits to 1 without affecting others.
- **Configuration of Flags**: Useful in configuring or activating specific bits in control registers.

Syntax

```
a |= b;
```

Syntax Explanation

- Each bit in a is compared to the corresponding bit in b.
- If either bit in a given position is 1, the result bit will be 1; otherwise, it will be 0.

Simple Code Example

```
int flags = 0b0010;    // Initial binary value: 0010
flags |= 0b1000;       // Now flags equals 1010 (sets bit 3 to 1)
```

Code Example Explanation

- The initial value of flags is 0b0010.
- After flags |= 0b1000, the value changes to 0b1010, setting the third bit from the right to 1.

Notes
Commonly used in microcontroller programming to activate specific features by setting configuration bits.

Warnings
Be mindful when using OR operations on variables that should only change certain bits.

---

8. Bitwise XOR Assignment (^=)

What is Bitwise XOR Assignment
The bitwise XOR assignment operator (^=) performs a bitwise exclusive OR (XOR) between two values and stores the result. The XOR operation is unique because it toggles bits: if the bits differ, the result is 1; otherwise, it is 0.

Use Purpose

- **Toggling Bits**: Ideal for inverting specific bits in a binary value, such as turning a feature on and off.
- **Bit Manipulation**: Enables dynamic control of individual bits without affecting others.

Syntax

```
a ^= b;
```

Syntax Explanation

- Each bit in a is XORed with the corresponding bit in b.
- The result bit is 1 if the two bits differ, and 0 if they are the same.

Simple Code Example

```
int flags = 0b1010;   // Initial binary value: 1010
flags ^= 0b1100;      // Now flags equals 0110 (toggles bits 3 and 2)
```

Code Example Explanation

- flags initially has the value 0b1010.
- After flags ^= 0b1100, bits 3 and 2 are toggled, resulting in 0b0110.

Notes
Useful for toggling specific bits in a register or flag variable.

Warnings
Repeated XOR on the same bits will revert them to the original value.

9. Left Shift Assignment (<<=)

What is Left Shift Assignment

The left shift assignment operator (<<=) shifts the bits in a variable to the left by a specified number of positions, padding the rightmost bits with zeros. Each left shift effectively multiplies the number by 2.

Use Purpose

- **Multiplication by Powers of Two**: Efficient way to multiply a number by 2^n.
- **Bit Manipulation**: Used in low-level programming for adjusting binary data.

Syntax

```
a <<= b;
```

Syntax Explanation

- a is shifted to the left by b positions.
- Bits shifted out on the left are discarded, and the rightmost positions are filled with zeros.

Simple Code Example

```
int value = 0b0001;   // Initial binary value: 0001
value <<= 2;          // Now value equals 0100 (shifted left by 2)
```

Code Example Explanation

- value is initially 0b0001.
- After value <<= 2, the bits shift left two positions, resulting in 0b0100, equivalent to multiplying by 4.

Notes

A simple and fast way to multiply by powers of two, commonly used in embedded programming.

10. Right Shift Assignment (>>=)

What is Right Shift Assignment

The right shift assignment operator (>>=) shifts the bits in a variable to the right by a specified number of positions, filling the leftmost bits with zeros. Each right shift effectively divides the number by 2.

Use Purpose

- **Division by Powers of Two**: Efficient way to divide by 2^n.
- **Bit Manipulation**: Useful for adjusting binary data, often in low-level operations.

Syntax

```
a >>= b;
```

Syntax Explanation

- a is shifted to the right by b positions.
- Bits shifted out on the right are discarded, and the leftmost positions are filled with zeros.

Simple Code Example

```
int value = 0b0100;   // Initial binary value: 0100
value >>= 2;          // Now value equals 0001 (shifted right by 2)
```

Code Example Explanation

- value starts as 0b0100.
- After value >>= 2, the bits shift right two positions, resulting in 0b0001, equivalent to dividing by 4.

Notes

Efficiently divides integers by powers of two, commonly used for downscaling values in embedded applications.

Warnings

Right-shifting signed integers can produce unexpected results depending on the platform, as it may fill leftmost bits with 1s instead of 0s.

Project Name

Binary Counter Display Using LEDs

Project Goal

To create a simple binary counter displayed on LEDs, with each LED representing one bit of a counter variable. The counter will utilize various compound operators to demonstrate their practical use in bit manipulation and arithmetic operations.

Requirement Components

- AVR Microcontroller (e.g., ATmega328P)
- LEDs for binary display
- Resistors (for current limiting)

Component Connection Table

Component	Microcontroller Pin	Additional Notes
LED1	PORTB0	Connect with resistor
LED2	PORTB1	Connect with resistor
LED3	PORTB2	Connect with resistor
LED4	PORTB3	Connect with resistor

Connection Analysis

Each LED is connected to a different pin on PORTB. The microcontroller will use compound operators to manipulate each LED by modifying the bits in the counter. The counter's binary value will be displayed on the LEDs, with each bit representing an LED's on/off state.

Program Software Setup

1. Open Atmel Studio and create a new project.
2. Configure the PORTB pins as outputs for controlling the LEDs.
3. Implement a loop to increment the counter variable and display its binary representation on the LEDs.

Project Code

```c
#include <avr/io.h>
#include <util/delay.h>

int main() {
    DDRB = 0xFF;   // Set all PORTB pins as output for LEDs

    uint8_t counter = 0;   // Initialize counter variable

    while(1) {
        PORTB = counter;   // Output the binary value of counter to
PORTB (LEDs)

        counter += 1;      // Increment counter using compound addition
assignment

        // Optional: Reset the counter using bitwise AND to keep it
within 4-bit range
        counter &= 0x0F;   // Counter will cycle from 0 to 15

        _delay_ms(500);    // Delay to make the counting visible on
LEDs
    }
}
```

Save and Run

1. Save and compile the code in Atmel Studio.
2. Program the microcontroller and observe the binary counting pattern displayed on the LEDs.

Check Output

Each LED will represent one bit of the counter variable, incrementing in binary (e.g., 0001, 0010, 0011, etc.). The counter will reset once it reaches 16 (0x10), cycling back to 0 to keep the display within the range of four LEDs.

Chapter-14 Math

Chapter Overview

Mathematical functions are essential in embedded systems programming for performing calculations, constraining values, and scaling inputs. In C, functions such as abs(), constrain(), map(), max(), min(), pow(), sq(), and sqrt() provide a foundation for mathematical operations on AVR microcontrollers. This chapter will cover these functions in detail, focusing on their syntax, use cases, and applications in embedded systems.

Chapter Goal

- Understand the purpose and usage of key mathematical functions in C.
- Learn how to perform absolute, scaling, constraining, and other mathematical operations.
- Apply these functions in a project to implement basic mathematical calculations on an AVR microcontroller.

Rules

- **Data Types**: Ensure appropriate data types (e.g., integers for min(), floats for sqrt()).
- **Function Arguments**: Use correct argument types to prevent unexpected results.
- **Math Library Inclusion**: Some functions require including the math.h library.
- **Precision**: Consider data type limitations (e.g., integer overflow, floating-point precision).

Brief Introduction to Math Functions in C

In C programming, several built-in functions provide powerful math capabilities, from basic absolute value calculations to complex exponentiation and square root operations. These functions are particularly useful in embedded applications where values must be constrained, scaled, or transformed to interact with physical sensors and actuators.

Syntax Table

Serial No	Function	Description	Syntax	Example
1	abs()	Returns the absolute value of an integer	`int abs(int x);`	`abs(-5);`
2	constrain()	Constrains a value within a range	`int constrain(int x, int min, int max);`	`constrain(10, 0, 5);`
3	map()	Maps a value from one range to another	`int map(int x, int in_min, int in_max, int out_min, int out_max);`	`map(10, 0, 20, 0, 100);`
4	max()	Returns the maximum of two values	`int max(int a, int b);`	`max(5, 10);`
5	min()	Returns the minimum of two values	`int min(int a, int b);`	`min(5, 10);`
6	pow()	Returns the result of a number raised to a power	`double pow(double base, double exp);`	`pow(2, 3);`

7	sq()	Squares a number	`int sq(int x);`	`sq(4);`
8	sqrt()	Returns the square root of a number	`double sqrt(double x);`	`sqrt(16);`

Detailed Breakdown for Each Function

1. Absolute Value: abs()

What is abs()
The abs() function returns the absolute value of an integer, converting any negative number to its positive equivalent.

Use Purpose

- **Removing Negative Signs**: Useful for distance calculations or ensuring positive values.
- **Handling Sensor Data**: Some sensors may produce negative readings that need to be treated as positive.

Syntax

```
int abs(int x);
```

Syntax Explanation

- **x**: Integer value to convert to its absolute form.
- Returns the absolute (positive) version of x.

Simple Code Example

```
int value = -10;
int absoluteValue = abs(value);   // absoluteValue now equals 10
```

Code Example Explanation

- Initializes value to -10.
- abs(value) returns 10, the absolute value of -10.

Notes

Only works with integers; for floating-point numbers, use `fabs()` from `math.h`.

Warnings

Not suitable for data types other than integers.

---

2. Constrain Value: `constrain()`

What is `constrain()`

The `constrain()` function limits a value to a specified range, ensuring that the value stays within a minimum and maximum bound.

Use Purpose

- **Clamping Values**: Keeps variables within safe ranges.
- **Input Validation**: Ensures sensor readings or calculations don't exceed limits.

Syntax

```
int constrain(int x, int min, int max);
```

Syntax Explanation

- **x**: Value to constrain.
- **min**: Minimum boundary for x.
- **max**: Maximum boundary for x.
- Returns x if within bounds, `min` if below `min`, and `max` if above `max`.

Simple Code Example

```
int constrainedValue = constrain(10, 0, 5);   // constrainedValue now equals 5
```

Code Example Explanation

- 10 is outside the range of 0 to 5, so `constrain()` returns 5.

Notes
Useful in cases where values must be limited to prevent errors.

Warnings
This function is not built-in for standard C, so you may need to define it manually.

---

3. Map Range: map()

What is map()
The map() function scales a value from one range to another, often used for translating sensor readings to meaningful values.

Use Purpose

- **Rescaling Values**: Converts sensor data to different ranges.
- **Calibration**: Maps raw data to usable output values.

Syntax

```
int map(int x, int in_min, int in_max, int out_min, int out_max);
```

Syntax Explanation

- **x**: Value to map.
- **in_min**: Minimum of input range.
- **in_max**: Maximum of input range.
- **out_min**: Minimum of output range.
- **out_max**: Maximum of output range.
- Returns x scaled to the output range.

Simple Code Example

```
int mappedValue = map(10, 0, 20, 0, 100);  // mappedValue now equals 50
```

Code Example Explanation

- Maps 10 from the range 0–20 to the range 0–100, resulting in 50.

Notes
Great for analog sensors where values need to be scaled.

Warnings
Ensure that `in_min` and `in_max` are not the same to avoid division by zero.

---

4. Maximum Value: `max()`

What is `max()`
The `max()` function returns the larger of two values.

Use Purpose

- **Comparisons**: Determine the higher of two numbers.
- **Input Validation**: Ensures a value doesn't fall below a threshold.

Syntax

```
int max(int a, int b);
```

Syntax Explanation

- **a**: First value.
- **b**: Second value.
- Returns the larger of a and b.

Simple Code Example

```
int maximumValue = max(5, 10);   // maximumValue now equals 10
```

Code Example Explanation

- Returns the larger value, 10, between 5 and 10.

Notes
A simple way to ensure a minimum threshold.

---

5. Minimum Value: `min()`

What is `min()`
The `min()` function returns the smaller of two values.

Use Purpose

- **Comparisons**: Determine the lower of two numbers.
- **Input Validation**: Ensures a value doesn't exceed a threshold.

Syntax

```
int min(int a, int b);
```

Syntax Explanation

- **a**: First value.
- **b**: Second value.
- Returns the smaller of a and b.

Simple Code Example

```
int minimumValue = min(5, 10);  // minimumValue now equals 5
```

Code Example Explanation

- Returns the smaller value, 5, between 5 and 10.

Notes
Useful for setting upper bounds on values.

Warnings
Only works with two values at a time.

6. Power Function: pow( )

What is pow( )
The pow( ) function raises a base to the power of an exponent.

Use Purpose

- **Exponential Calculations**: Useful for polynomial and scientific calculations.
- **Scaling Factors**: Often used in geometric transformations.

Syntax

```
double pow(double base, double exp);
```

Syntax Explanation

- **base**: The number to be raised.
- **exp**: The exponent.
- Returns base raised to the power of exp.

Simple Code Example

```
double result = pow(2, 3);  // result now equals 8
```

Code Example Explanation

- Calculates 2 raised to the power of 3, which is 8.

Notes
Requires math.h.

Warnings
Using high exponents may lead to overflow.

7. Square Function: sq( )

What is sq( )
The sq( ) function squares a number (i.e., multiplies it by itself).

Use Purpose

- **Calculations**: Efficient for squaring values in mathematical formulas.

Syntax

```
int sq(int x);
```

Syntax Explanation

- **x**: The integer to square.
- Returns x squared.

Simple Code Example

```
int squaredValue = sq(4);  // squaredValue now equals 16
```

Code Example Explanation

- Returns 4 * 4 = 16.

Notes
Custom function in some environments; you may need to define it.

Warnings
Watch for overflow in small data types.

8. Square Root: sqrt()

What is sqrt()

The sqrt() function calculates the square root of a number.

Use Purpose

- **Mathematical Calculations**: Used in distance, geometry, and physics calculations.

Syntax

```
double sqrt(double x);
```

Syntax Explanation

- x: The number to find the square root of.
- Returns the square root of x.

Simple Code Example

```
double rootValue = sqrt(16);   // rootValue now equals 4
```

Code Example Explanation

- Returns the square root of 16, which is 4.

Notes

Requires math.h.

Warnings

For non-negative inputs only; negative values return NaN.

Relevant Project Section

Project Name
Temperature Converter with Scaled and Constrained Output

Project Goal
Use math functions to create a temperature converter that reads a raw temperature value, maps it to a Celsius scale, constrains it, and calculates derived values like square roots.

Requirement Components

- AVR Microcontroller (e.g., ATmega328P)
- Temperature sensor (e.g., LM35)
- Serial monitor for output display

Component Connection Table

Component	Microcontroller Pin	Additional Notes
Temperature Sensor	ADC pin	Connect to analog input
Serial Interface	TX, RX	For displaying results

Connection Analysis
The temperature sensor connects to the ADC input pin, and readings are processed using math functions to convert and scale values.

Program Software Setup

1. Open Atmel Studio and create a new project.
2. Configure ADC input for temperature reading and set up serial communication.

Project Code

```c
#include <avr/io.h>
#include <util/delay.h>
#include <math.h>
#include <stdio.h>

// Placeholder functions for map and constrain if needed
int constrain(int x, int min, int max) {
    if (x < min) return min;
    if (x > max) return max;
    return x;
}

int map(int x, int in_min, int in_max, int out_min, int out_max) {
    return (x - in_min) * (out_max - out_min) / (in_max - in_min) +
out_min;
}

int main() {
    int rawTemp = 200; // Simulated ADC value
    int tempCelsius = map(rawTemp, 0, 1023, -40, 125);
    tempCelsius = constrain(tempCelsius, -40, 125);

    printf("Temperature (C): %d\n", tempCelsius);
    printf("Absolute Temp: %d\n", abs(tempCelsius));
    printf("Temperature Squared: %d\n", sq(tempCelsius));
    printf("Square Root of Temp: %.2f\n", sqrt(tempCelsius));
}
```

Save and Run

1. Save and compile the code in Atmel Studio.
2. Run the program to see processed values displayed in the serial monitor.

Chapter-15 Characters

Chapter Overview

Characters are essential in C programming for representing letters, digits, and symbols in a readable format. In C, characters are represented using the char data type, which stores ASCII values corresponding to readable symbols. Handling characters is particularly useful for user interfaces, serial communication, and text processing on AVR microcontrollers. This chapter will cover character handling, ASCII values, and useful character functions for AVR programming.

Chapter Goal

- Understand the role of characters in C and how they're represented using ASCII.
- Learn to perform basic character manipulations, including conversions between uppercase and lowercase.
- Apply character operations in a simple project that uses serial communication.

Rules

- **Data Type**: Characters in C are stored in the char data type, occupying 1 byte (8 bits).
- **ASCII Values**: Each character corresponds to a unique ASCII value (e.g., 'A' = 65).
- **Character Functions**: The ctype.h library provides functions for checking and converting character types.
- **Null-Terminated Strings**: In C, strings are arrays of characters ending with a null character (' \0 ').

Brief Introduction to Characters in C

Characters in C are typically stored as 8-bit integers, each representing an ASCII code for letters, digits, and symbols. By storing and manipulating these codes, we can display text, process user inputs, and communicate data in a human-readable format. This approach is beneficial in embedded programming for working with serial interfaces or creating basic textual displays.

Syntax Table

Serial No	Topic	Syntax	Example
1	Character Declaration	`char ch = 'A';`	`char letter = 'B';`
2	ASCII Value Assignment	`char ch = 65;`	`char digit = 48;`
3	Character Array (String)	`char str[] = "Hello";`	`char name[] = "AVR";`
4	Character Functions	`isalpha(char), toupper(char)`	`isalpha('A')` returns 1

Detailed Breakdown for Each Concept

1. Character Declaration and Initialization

What is Character Declaration
In C, characters are declared using the `char` data type. A `char` variable can store a single ASCII character by using either a character literal (e.g., `'A'`) or an ASCII value (e.g., `65`).

Use Purpose

- **Text Display**: Display letters and symbols on a screen or serial monitor.
- **Input Processing**: Handle individual characters from user input.

Syntax

```
char ch = 'A';
```

Syntax Explanation

- **char ch**: Declares a variable ch of type char.
- **'A'**: Assigns the character literal A to ch. Alternatively, ch could be assigned the ASCII code 65.

Simple Code Example

```
char letter = 'B';  // Declares a char variable with value 'B'
```

Code Example Explanation

- The letter variable stores the character B (ASCII value 66).

Notes

Characters can be assigned ASCII values directly (e.g., char ch = 65; for A).

Warnings

Character literals must be enclosed in single quotes (e.g., 'A', not "A").

---

2. ASCII Value Assignment

What is ASCII Value Assignment

ASCII (American Standard Code for Information Interchange) assigns a unique integer to each character, such as 65 for 'A' and 97 for 'a'. Assigning ASCII values to char variables allows us to manipulate characters numerically.

Use Purpose

- **Direct ASCII Manipulation**: Work with specific ASCII codes for greater control.
- **Numeric Comparisons**: Perform operations based on ASCII ranges.

Syntax

```
char ch = 65;
```

Syntax Explanation

- **char ch**: Declares a variable ch of type char.
- **65**: Assigns the ASCII value 65 (corresponding to A) to ch.

Simple Code Example

```
char digit = 48;  // '0' in ASCII
```

Code Example Explanation

- The digit variable is assigned 48, the ASCII value for '0'.

Notes
Useful for conversions and comparisons by numeric ASCII codes.

Warnings
Ensure values are within the ASCII range for characters (0–127).

---

3. Character Arrays (Strings)

What are Character Arrays
Strings in C are represented as arrays of char elements. Each character in the array is stored sequentially, and the string ends with a null character (' \0 '), signaling the end of the text.

Use Purpose

- **Storing Text**: Store and manipulate sequences of characters.
- **Message Display**: Use strings to display longer messages on a screen or serial monitor.

Syntax

```
char str[] = "Hello";
```

Syntax Explanation

- **char str[]**: Declares an array str that can hold multiple characters.
- **"Hello"**: Initializes str with the characters 'H', 'e', 'l', 'l', 'o', and a null character ('\0') automatically.

Simple Code Example

```
char name[] = "AVR";
```

Code Example Explanation

- Creates a character array name storing the string "AVR".

Notes
Strings require an extra null character at the end, handled automatically when using double quotes.

Warnings
String arrays must be sized appropriately to hold the entire string, including the null character.

---

4. Character Functions in ctype.h

What are Character Functions
The ctype.h library in C provides functions for character classification (e.g., isalpha(), isdigit()) and conversion (e.g., toupper(), tolower()), which simplify processing characters based on type and case.

Use Purpose

- **Character Checking**: Determine if a character is alphabetic, numeric, etc.
- **Case Conversion**: Convert characters to uppercase or lowercase.

Syntax

```
int isalpha(char c);
char toupper(char c);
```

Syntax Explanation

- **isalpha(char c)**: Returns non-zero if c is an alphabetic letter; otherwise, returns zero.
- **toupper(char c)**: Converts c to uppercase if it's lowercase; otherwise, it returns c unchanged.

Simple Code Example

```
char ch = 'a';
if (isalpha(ch)) {
    ch = toupper(ch);   // ch is now 'A'
}
```

Code Example Explanation

- Checks if ch is alphabetic, then converts it to uppercase using toupper().

Notes

The ctype.h library provides useful functions for handling and modifying characters.

Warnings

Functions like isalpha() return non-zero for true, which may vary between systems.

Relevant Project Section

Project Name
Serial Character Processing and Display

Project Goal
Use character handling to create a simple program that reads characters from the serial port, processes them, and displays uppercase or lowercase versions.

Requirement Components

- AVR Microcontroller (e.g., ATmega328P)
- Serial monitor for character input/output

Component Connection Table

Component	Microcontroller Pin	Additional Notes
Serial Interface	TX, RX	For reading and writing characters

Connection Analysis
The serial interface connects to the microcontroller's TX and RX pins, enabling communication with a terminal or serial monitor on a computer. This allows the microcontroller to read characters sent via the serial port and display processed versions back to the terminal.

Program Software Setup

1. Open Atmel Studio and create a new project.
2. Configure UART for serial communication.
3. Set up `ctype.h` for character processing.

Project Code

```c
#include <avr/io.h>
#include <ctype.h>
#include <util/delay.h>
#include <stdio.h>

// Function to initialize UART for serial communication
void UART_init(unsigned int baud) {
    unsigned int ubrr = F_CPU/16/baud-1;
    UBRR0H = (unsigned char)(ubrr>>8);
    UBRR0L = (unsigned char)ubrr;
    UCSR0B = (1<<RXEN0) | (1<<TXEN0); // Enable receiver and
transmitter
    UCSR0C = (1<<USBS0) | (3<<UCSZ00); // Set frame format: 8 data
bits, 2 stop bits
}

// Function to transmit a character over UART
void UART_transmit(char data) {
    while (!( UCSR0A & (1<<UDRE0))); // Wait for empty transmit buffer
    UDR0 = data; // Put data into buffer, sends the data
}

// Function to receive a character over UART
char UART_receive(void) {
    while (!(UCSR0A & (1<<RXC0))); // Wait for data to be received
    return UDR0; // Get and return received data from buffer
}

// Function to transmit a string over UART
void UART_printString(const char* str) {
    while(*str) {
        UART_transmit(*str++);
    }
}

int main(void) {
    UART_init(9600); // Initialize UART with 9600 baud rate

    UART_printString("Enter a character: \n");

    while (1) {
        char received_char = UART_receive(); // Receive a character
from serial port

        if (isalpha(received_char)) { // Check if the character is
alphabetic
            if (islower(received_char)) {
                received_char = toupper(received_char); // Convert to
uppercase
                UART_printString("Uppercase: ");
            } else {
                received_char = tolower(received_char); // Convert to
lowercase
```

```
            UART_printString("Lowercase: ");
        }
    } else {
        UART_printString("Non-alphabetic character received: ");
    }

    UART_transmit(received_char); // Send processed character back
over serial
    UART_transmit('\n'); // Newline for better readability
    }
}
```

Save and Run

1. Save and compile the code in Atmel Studio.
2. Upload the code to the microcontroller.
3. Open a serial monitor, set to the correct baud rate (9600),
   and test character processing by sending letters and
   observing the case conversions or other output responses.

Check Output

- When an alphabetic character is sent, the microcontroller
  should convert it to the opposite case and send it back with a
  message indicating the transformation.
- For non-alphabetic characters, a message will indicate that a
  non-alphabetic character was received.

Chapter-16 Communication

Chapter Overview

Communication is essential in embedded systems to exchange data between microcontrollers, sensors, and peripherals. AVR microcontrollers support multiple communication protocols, including UART (Universal Asynchronous Receiver/Transmitter), SPI (Serial Peripheral Interface), and I2C (Inter-Integrated Circuit). This chapter will introduce these protocols, explain their configuration in C, and demonstrate practical examples using Atmel Studio.

Chapter Goal

- Understand UART, SPI, and I2C communication protocols.
- Learn to set up and configure each protocol in C for AVR microcontrollers.
- Complete a project using UART communication to send and receive data from a serial monitor.

Rules

- **Protocol Selection**: Choose the appropriate protocol based on speed, distance, and number of devices.
- **Baud Rate and Clock Speed**: Ensure correct settings for baud rate (UART) and clock speed (SPI, I2C).
- **Data Format**: Configure data frames (e.g., 8-bit data, parity bits) based on the application.
- **Connections**: Verify wiring for each communication type (e.g., TX/RX for UART, SCK/MOSI/MISO/SS for SPI, and SDA/SCL for I2C).

Brief Introduction to Communication Protocols in AVR

AVR microcontrollers support various communication protocols, each suitable for different types of applications. UART is commonly used for serial communication with computers and GPS modules, SPI is fast and ideal for short-distance communication with multiple devices, and I2C is effective for connecting multiple devices over a two-wire bus.

Syntax Table

Serial No	Protocol	Common Functions	Example Usage
1	UART	`UART_init()`, `UART_transmit()`, `UART_receive()`	Serial monitor communication
2	SPI	`SPI_init()`, `SPI_send()`, `SPI_receive()`	Sensor communication
3	I2C	`I2C_init()`, `I2C_start()`, `I2C_write()`, `I2C_read()`	Connecting multiple peripherals

Detailed Breakdown for Each Protocol

1. UART Communication

What is UART

UART (Universal Asynchronous Receiver/Transmitter) is a serial communication protocol used for simple and effective data exchange between a microcontroller and devices like computers, Bluetooth modules, or GPS modules. UART communication is asynchronous, meaning it doesn't require a shared clock signal between devices.

Use Purpose

- **Data Logging**: Send sensor data to a computer for monitoring.
- **User Interface**: Display messages or receive commands from a serial terminal.

Syntax

```
void UART_init(unsigned int baud);
void UART_transmit(char data);
char UART_receive(void);
```

Syntax Explanation

- **UART_init(unsigned int baud)**: Configures the UART communication with a specified baud rate.
- **UART_transmit(char data)**: Sends a single character over UART.
- **UART_receive(void)**: Waits for and receives a single character from UART.

Simple Code Example

```
UART_init(9600);        // Initialize UART with 9600 baud rate
UART_transmit('H');    // Transmit character 'H'
char received = UART_receive(); // Receive a character
```

Code Example Explanation

- Initializes UART at 9600 baud.
- Transmits 'H' and receives a character from the connected device.

Notes
Set the same baud rate on both the microcontroller and the external device for reliable communication.

Warnings
Incorrect baud rate configuration can result in data corruption.

---

2. SPI Communication

What is SPI
SPI (Serial Peripheral Interface) is a synchronous serial communication protocol used for high-speed data transfer over short distances. It's typically used to communicate with sensors, displays,

and other peripherals. SPI operates using four lines: MISO, MOSI, SCK, and SS.

Use Purpose

- **Sensor Data**: Exchange data with high-speed sensors.
- **Display Control**: Send display data to an LCD or OLED screen.

Syntax

```
void SPI_init(void);
void SPI_send(char data);
char SPI_receive(void);
```

Syntax Explanation

- **SPI_init(void)**: Configures the microcontroller as either an SPI master or slave.
- **SPI_send(char data)**: Sends a byte of data to an SPI-connected device.
- **SPI_receive(void)**: Receives a byte of data from an SPI device.

Simple Code Example

```
SPI_init();           // Initialize SPI as master
SPI_send(0x45);       // Send data (0x45) to SPI device
char data = SPI_receive(); // Receive data from SPI device
```

Code Example Explanation

- Initializes the microcontroller as an SPI master.
- Sends 0x45 to the connected SPI device and receives a byte in return.

Notes
Only one device can communicate at a time using SPI; manage the
SS pin to select devices.

Warnings
Ensure MISO/MOSI are connected correctly, or data transmission
may fail.

3. I2C Communication

What is I2C
I2C (Inter-Integrated Circuit) is a two-wire synchronous
communication protocol used for connecting multiple peripherals. It
uses two lines, SDA (data) and SCL (clock), allowing multiple
devices to share the same bus.

Use Purpose

- **Sensor Networks**: Communicate with multiple sensors on
  the same bus.
- **EEPROM Communication**: Read/write data from an
  external EEPROM.

Syntax

```
void I2C_init(void);
void I2C_start(void);
void I2C_write(char data);
char I2C_read(void);
```

Syntax Explanation

- **I2C_init(void)**: Sets up I2C communication, including
  setting the clock frequency.
- **I2C_start(void)**: Generates a start condition on the I2C
  bus.
- **I2C_write(char data)**: Sends a byte of data over the
  I2C bus.
- **I2C_read(void)**: Reads a byte of data from the I2C bus.

Simple Code Example

```
I2C_init();          // Initialize I2C
I2C_start();         // Start I2C communication
I2C_write(0x50);     // Send address and data to I2C device
char data = I2C_read(); // Read data from I2C device
```

Code Example Explanation

- Initializes I2C communication.
- Starts communication, sends an address, writes data, and reads back a response.

Notes
I2C allows multiple devices to communicate, so each device must have a unique address.

Warnings
Address conflicts can disrupt communication.

Relevant Project Section

Project Name
Serial Communication Using UART

Project Goal
Create a simple program that uses UART to send and receive messages between the microcontroller and a serial monitor on a computer.

Requirement Components

- AVR Microcontroller (e.g., ATmega328P)
- USB-to-UART adapter or serial port for connecting to a computer
- Serial monitor on a PC (e.g., Putty or Arduino Serial Monitor)

Component Connection Table

Component	Microcontroller Pin	Additional Notes
USB-to-UART Adapter	TX, RX	Connect TX to RX and RX to TX

Connection Analysis

The microcontroller's TX pin connects to the RX pin on the USB-to-UART adapter, and vice versa, enabling full-duplex communication with a computer. The serial monitor will be used to send commands and view responses from the microcontroller.

Program Software Setup

1. Open Atmel Studio and create a new project.
2. Configure UART for 9600 baud communication.
3. Implement functions to send and receive data over UART.

Project Code

```c
#include <avr/io.h>
#include <util/delay.h>
#include <stdio.h>

// Function to initialize UART for serial communication
void UART_init(unsigned int baud) {
    unsigned int ubrr = F_CPU/16/baud-1;
    UBRR0H = (unsigned char)(ubrr>>8);
    UBRR0L = (unsigned char)ubrr;
    UCSR0B = (1<<RXEN0) | (1<<TXEN0); // Enable receiver and
transmitter
    UCSR0C = (1<<USBS0) | (3<<UCSZ00); // Set frame format: 8 data
bits, 2 stop bits
}

// Function to transmit a character over UART
void UART_transmit(char data) {
    while (!( UCSR0A & (1<<UDRE0))); // Wait for empty transmit buffer
    UDR0 = data; // Put data into buffer, sends the data
}

// Function to receive a character over UART
char UART_receive(void) {
    while (!(UCSR0A & (1<<RXC0))); // Wait for data to be received
    return UDR0; // Get and return received data from buffer
}
```

```c
// Function to transmit a string over UART
void UART_printString(const char* str) {
    while(*str) {
        UART_transmit(*str++);
    }
}

int main(void) {
    UART_init(9600); // Initialize UART with 9600 baud rate
    UART_printString("Enter a character:\n");

    while (1) {
        char received_char = UART_receive(); // Receive a character
from serial port
        UART_transmit(received_char); // Echo back the received
character
        UART_printString("\nReceived character: ");
        UART_transmit(received_char);
        UART_transmit('\n'); // Newline for better readability
    }
}
```

Save and Run

1. Save and compile the code in Atmel Studio.
2. Upload the code to the microcontroller.
3. Open a serial monitor on the computer set to 9600 baud rate, and type characters to test UART communication.

Check Output

- When a character is sent from the serial monitor, the microcontroller will echo it back and display a message confirming the received character.

Chapter-17 Bluetooth Communication

Overview

Bluetooth communication enables wireless data exchange between microcontrollers and Bluetooth-enabled devices like smartphones, tablets, and computers. AVR microcontrollers typically communicate with Bluetooth modules using UART. Modules like the HC-05 or HC-06 make Bluetooth integration simple, providing a wireless link with no need for extra wiring. This section will cover how to set up UART communication for Bluetooth, configure Bluetooth modules, and create a simple program to send and receive data over Bluetooth.

Goal

- Understand how to set up a Bluetooth module with an AVR microcontroller.
- Configure UART communication for Bluetooth data exchange.
- Complete a project that enables wireless data transmission between a microcontroller and a Bluetooth-enabled device.

Requirements

- **Bluetooth Module (e.g., HC-05/HC-06)**: Provides Bluetooth communication capability with UART support.
- **AVR Microcontroller (e.g., ATmega328P)**: Handles UART communication with the Bluetooth module.
- **Bluetooth Terminal App**: Used on a smartphone or computer to send and receive data wirelessly with the Bluetooth module.

Rules

- **UART Baud Rate**: Set the baud rate to match the default baud rate of the Bluetooth module (usually 9600 or 38400).
- **Wiring**: Connect the module's TX to the microcontroller's RX and vice versa.
- **Bluetooth Configuration**: If necessary, configure the Bluetooth module for pairing, mode, and baud rate before use.
- **Power Supply**: Ensure the Bluetooth module operates at a safe voltage level (e.g., 3.3V or 5V depending on the module).

Setting Up the Bluetooth Module

Bluetooth modules typically support AT commands to configure settings such as name, baud rate, and pairing PIN. These settings can be configured by connecting the Bluetooth module to the microcontroller's UART and issuing AT commands. However, in many cases, the default settings work well for basic communication tasks.

Example AT Commands for Configuration

- **AT**: Checks if the module is responsive.
- **AT+NAME=YourDeviceName**: Sets the Bluetooth name.
- **AT+PIN=1234**: Sets the Bluetooth pairing PIN.
- **AT+BAUD4**: Sets the baud rate to 9600 (varies depending on module).

Basic Wiring

Bluetooth Module Pin	Microcontroller Pin	Notes
VCC	5V or 3.3V	Power supply
GND	GND	Ground connection
TXD	RX	Transmit line to receive line

RXD	TX	Receive line to transmit line

Implementing Bluetooth Communication Using UART

1. UART Initialization for Bluetooth
Since the Bluetooth module communicates over UART, configure the microcontroller's UART for serial communication at the appropriate baud rate (often 9600 bps). Once configured, the microcontroller can send and receive data wirelessly through the Bluetooth module.

Syntax

```
void UART_init(unsigned int baud);
void UART_transmit(char data);
char UART_receive(void);
```

Syntax Explanation

- **UART_init(unsigned int baud)**: Sets up UART communication for the specified baud rate.
- **UART_transmit(char data)**: Sends a character over UART, which will be transmitted wirelessly via Bluetooth.
- **UART_receive(void)**: Receives a character over UART from the Bluetooth module.

Example Code for Bluetooth Communication

This example sets up UART communication to send and receive data with a Bluetooth module, echoing received characters back to the connected Bluetooth device.

```
#include <avr/io.h>
#include <util/delay.h>
#include <stdio.h>

// Initialize UART
void UART_init(unsigned int baud) {
    unsigned int ubrr = F_CPU/16/baud-1;
    UBRR0H = (unsigned char)(ubrr>>8);
    UBRR0L = (unsigned char)ubrr;
```

```c
    UCSR0B = (1<<RXEN0) | (1<<TXEN0); // Enable receiver and
transmitter
    UCSR0C = (1<<USBS0) | (3<<UCSZ00); // Set frame format: 8 data
bits, 2 stop bits
}

// Transmit a single character over UART
void UART_transmit(char data) {
    while (!(UCSR0A & (1<<UDRE0))); // Wait for empty transmit buffer
    UDR0 = data; // Put data into buffer, sends the data
}

// Receive a single character over UART
char UART_receive(void) {
    while (!(UCSR0A & (1<<RXC0))); // Wait for data to be received
    return UDR0; // Get and return received data from buffer
}
// Transmit a string over UART
void UART_printString(const char* str) {
    while(*str) {
        UART_transmit(*str++);
    }
}
int main(void) {
    UART_init(9600); // Initialize UART with 9600 baud rate for
Bluetooth

    UART_printString("Bluetooth Communication Ready\n");

    while (1) {
        char received_char = UART_receive(); // Receive a character
from Bluetooth
        UART_printString("Received: ");
        UART_transmit(received_char); // Echo received character back
        UART_transmit('\n'); // Newline for readability
    }
}
```

Save and Run

1. Save and compile the code in Atmel Studio.
2. Upload the code to the microcontroller.
3. Pair the Bluetooth module with a smartphone or computer using a Bluetooth terminal app.
4. Set the app to the same baud rate (9600) and start sending characters to the microcontroller.

Check Output

- When a character is sent from the Bluetooth terminal, the microcontroller will receive it, echo it back, and print it with a message "Received: X".
- The system allows real-time communication, useful for remote control or monitoring applications.

Chapter-18 Functions

Chapter Overview
Functions are fundamental in C programming for structuring code into reusable, organized blocks. In embedded programming, functions help modularize code for readability, maintainability, and efficiency. This chapter will cover defining, declaring, and calling functions in C, with a focus on AVR microcontroller programming in Atmel Studio. Through examples, we'll explore how functions can simplify complex operations and facilitate code reuse.

Chapter Goal
- Understand how to define and use functions in C.
- Learn to pass parameters and return values from functions.
- Apply functions in a practical project to modularize microcontroller code.

Rules
- **Function Declaration**: Every function should have a declaration (prototype) before it is used, specifying its return type and parameters.
- **Return Types**: Functions can return a value (e.g., `int`, `float`) or `void` if they do not return anything.
- **Parameters**: Parameters allow functions to accept input values for processing.
- **Scope**: Variables declared within a function are local to that function.

Brief Introduction to Functions in C
A function is a block of code designed to perform a specific task, defined with a name, parameters, and a return type. Functions help encapsulate logic into reusable blocks, enabling efficient program organization and reducing redundancy. In embedded systems, functions are especially useful for organizing code related to hardware control, sensor reading, or data processing.

Syntax Table

Serial No	Topic	Syntax	Example
1	Function Declaration	`return_type function_name(parameters);`	`int add(int a, int b);`
2	Function Definition	`return_type function_name(parameters) { ... }`	`int add(int a, int b) { ... }`
3	Function Call	`function_name(arguments);`	`add(2, 3);`
4	Returning a Value	`return expression;`	`return a + b;`

Detailed Breakdown for Each Concept

1. Function Declaration

What is Function Declaration
A function declaration, also called a function prototype, specifies the function's return type, name, and parameters. Declarations are typically placed at the beginning of a program or in a header file to inform the compiler about the function's existence before it is called.

Use Purpose

- **Inform the Compiler**: Allows the compiler to check function calls for correct usage.
- **Organize Code**: Provides a clear structure by listing available functions.

Syntax

```
return_type function_name(parameter_type1 parameter1, parameter_type2
parameter2);
```

Syntax Explanation

- **`return_type`**: Specifies the type of value the function returns (e.g., `int`, `void` if it doesn't return a value).
- **`function_name`**: The unique identifier for the function.
- **`parameter_type`** and **`parameter`**: Define the types and names of parameters that the function accepts.

Simple Code Example

```
int add(int a, int b);   // Declares a function that adds two integers
```

Code Example Explanation

- Declares a function named `add` that takes two `int` parameters and returns an `int`.

Notes
A function declaration ends with a semicolon (`;`).

---

2. Function Definition

What is Function Definition
The function definition contains the actual code that performs the function's task. It includes the function header (return type, name, parameters) followed by the function body enclosed in curly braces (`{ ... }`).

Use Purpose

- **Implement Logic**: Defines the actions performed when the function is called.
- **Encapsulate Code**: Allows reuse of common logic in multiple places.

Syntax

```
return_type function_name(parameter_type1 parameter1, parameter_type2
parameter2) {
    // Code to perform the function's task
    return value;   // if return_type is not void
}
```

Syntax Explanation

- **return_type**: Defines the type of the function's return value.
- **function_name**: Unique name used to call the function.
- **parameter_type** and **parameter**: Parameters are used as inputs within the function.
- **return**: Returns a value if return_type is not void.

Simple Code Example

```
int add(int a, int b) {
    return a + b;
}
```

Code Example Explanation

- Defines a function add that takes two int parameters, adds them, and returns the result.

Notes
A function with a void return type does not need a return statement.

---

3. Function Call

What is Function Call
A function call invokes the function to execute its code. Function calls include the function's name followed by parentheses containing any necessary arguments.

Use Purpose

- **Execute the Function**: Runs the code inside the function.
- **Pass Arguments**: Provides values for the function's parameters.

Syntax

```
function_name(arguments);
```

Syntax Explanation

- **function_name**: The name of the function to call.
- **arguments**: Values provided to the function's parameters.

Simple Code Example

```
int result = add(2, 3);  // Calls the function add with arguments 2 and 3
```

Code Example Explanation

- Calls add with 2 and 3 as arguments and stores the returned value in result.

Notes

The number and types of arguments must match the function's parameters.

---

4. Returning a Value
What is Returning a Value

When a function completes its task, it can return a value to the calling code using the return statement. The type of value returned must match the function's return type.

Use Purpose

- **Provide Output**: Returns results for further processing.
- **End Function Execution**: The return statement ends the function.

Syntax

```
return expression;
```

Syntax Explanation

- **return**: A keyword that signals the end of the function and specifies the output.
- **expression**: The value or variable to return, matching the function's return type.

Simple Code Example

```
return a + b;  // Returns the sum of a and b to the calling function
```

Code Example Explanation

- The function completes and returns the value of a + b to the caller.

Notes

A void function does not use return with a value.

Relevant Project Section

Project Name

Temperature Conversion Function with Serial Output

Project Goal

Create a program that uses a function to convert a temperature from Celsius to Fahrenheit, demonstrating function calls, parameter passing, and serial output.

Requirement Components

- AVR Microcontroller (e.g., ATmega328P)
- Serial monitor for displaying the result

Component Connection Table

Component	Microcontroller Pin	Additional Notes
Serial Interface	TX, RX	For displaying temperature

Connection Analysis

The microcontroller communicates with a serial monitor over the TX and RX pins to display the converted temperature in Fahrenheit.

Program Software Setup

1. Open Atmel Studio and create a new project.
2. Configure UART for serial communication.
3. Implement a function to perform the Celsius-to-Fahrenheit conversion.

Project Code

```c
#include <avr/io.h>
#include <util/delay.h>
#include <stdio.h>

// Function to initialize UART for serial communication
void UART_init(unsigned int baud) {
    unsigned int ubrr = F_CPU/16/baud-1;
    UBRR0H = (unsigned char)(ubrr>>8);
    UBRR0L = (unsigned char)ubrr;
    UCSR0B = (1<<RXEN0) | (1<<TXEN0);
    UCSR0C = (1<<USBS0) | (3<<UCSZ00);
}

// Function to transmit a character over UART
void UART_transmit(char data) {
    while (!(UCSR0A & (1<<UDRE0)));
    UDR0 = data;
}

// Function to transmit a string over UART
void UART_printString(const char* str) {
    while(*str) {
        UART_transmit(*str++);
    }
}

// Function to convert Celsius to Fahrenheit
```

```
float celsiusToFahrenheit(float celsius) {
    return (celsius * 9 / 5) + 32;
}

int main(void) {
    UART_init(9600); // Initialize UART with 9600 baud rate

    float celsius = 25.0; // Example temperature in Celsius
    float fahrenheit = celsiusToFahrenheit(celsius); // Call conversion
function

    char buffer[20];
    snprintf(buffer, sizeof(buffer), "Fahrenheit: %.2f\n", fahrenheit);

    UART_printString(buffer); // Print the converted temperature
    while(1);
}
```

Save and Run

1. Save and compile the code in Atmel Studio.
2. Upload the code to the microcontroller.
3. Open a serial monitor and observe the temperature in Fahrenheit displayed.

Check Output

- The serial monitor should display "Fahrenheit: 77.00" for a Celsius input of 25.0. The function celsiusToFahrenheit performs the conversion, demonstrating modular code with reusable functionality.

Chapter-19 Variable Scope

Chapter Overview
Variable scope refers to the region within a program where a variable is accessible. Understanding scope is essential for writing efficient, error-free programs in C, particularly in embedded programming with AVR microcontrollers. Scope affects memory usage, variable accessibility, and program behavior. This chapter will cover the types of scope (global, local, and static) and how to apply them in practical programming scenarios.

Chapter Goal

- Understand the different types of variable scope in C.
- Learn to use local, global, and static variables effectively.
- Apply variable scope knowledge in a project to manage memory and access control in embedded code.

Rules

- **Local Scope**: Variables declared inside a function or block are accessible only within that function or block.
- **Global Scope**: Variables declared outside any function are accessible throughout the program.
- **Static Scope**: Static variables retain their value between function calls and are limited to the file or function where they are declared.
- **Lifetime**: Scope determines not only visibility but also the variable's lifetime in memory.

Brief Introduction to Variable Scope in C
In C, scope determines the part of the program where a variable can be accessed. Variables can have local scope (visible only within a function), global scope (visible throughout the file), or static scope (persistent within its defined scope). Understanding scope helps manage memory efficiently and avoid conflicts or unexpected results in embedded programs.

Syntax Table

Seria l No	Topic	Syntax	Example
1	Local Variable	`int localVar = 5;` (inside function)	`int sum(int x) { int localVar; }`
2	Global Variable	`int globalVar = 10;` (outside functions)	`int globalVar = 10;`
3	Static Local Variable	`static int count = 0;`	`static int counter;`

Detailed Breakdown for Each Type of Scope

1. Local Scope (Function Scope)

What is Local Scope
Variables declared within a function or block (enclosed in {}) are local to that function or block. Local variables are created when the function is called and destroyed when the function exits, freeing up memory.

Use Purpose

- **Temporary Storage**: Store data temporarily for calculations or processing within a function.
- **Memory Efficiency**: Local variables are allocated and deallocated dynamically, reducing memory usage.

Syntax

```
void myFunction() {
    int localVar = 5;
    // localVar is accessible only within myFunction
}
```

Syntax Explanation

- **int localVar**: Declares a variable named `localVar` within `myFunction`.
- **Scope**: `localVar` is accessible only within the function `myFunction` and does not exist outside it.

Simple Code Example

```
int add(int a, int b) {
    int sum = a + b;  // sum is local to add()
    return sum;
}
```

Code Example Explanation

- The variable `sum` is defined within `add` and exists only for the duration of this function call.

Notes
Local variables help keep functions independent and prevent conflicts with variables in other parts of the code.

Warnings
Attempting to access a local variable outside its function results in a compilation error.

---

2. Global Scope (File Scope)

What is Global Scope
A global variable is declared outside any function, usually at the top of the file. Global variables are accessible by all functions within that file and retain their value for the program's duration.

Use Purpose
- **Data Sharing**: Allows multiple functions to access and modify a single variable.
- **Persistent Data**: Stores values that need to be retained throughout program execution.

Syntax

```
int globalVar = 10;

void someFunction() {
    globalVar += 5;   // Accessible here
}

void anotherFunction() {
    globalVar = 20;   // Also accessible here
}
```

Syntax Explanation

- **int globalVar = 10;**: Declares a variable globalVar at the file level, making it accessible to all functions in the file.
- **Scope**: globalVar is accessible within any function in the file.

Simple Code Example

```
int counter = 0;

void increment() {
    counter++;
}

void reset() {
    counter = 0;
}
```

Code Example Explanation

- counter is a global variable accessible and modifiable by increment() and reset().

Notes
Global variables help share data across functions but should be used sparingly to avoid unintended modifications.

Warnings
Excessive use of global variables can lead to code that's difficult to debug and maintain.

3. Static Local Scope

What is Static Local Scope

A static local variable is declared with the `static` keyword inside a function. Unlike regular local variables, static local variables retain their value between function calls but are only accessible within that function.

Use Purpose

- **Persistent Local Data**: Retain a variable's value across function calls.
- **Encapsulation**: Limits access to the variable while retaining its value within the function.

Syntax

```
void myFunction() {
    static int counter = 0;
    counter++;  // Retains its value between calls to myFunction
}
```

Syntax Explanation

- **`static int counter = 0;`**: Declares counter as a static variable within myFunction.
- **Persistence**: counter is initialized only once and retains its value for each subsequent call to myFunction.

Simple Code Example

```
void callCount() {
    static int count = 0;
    count++;
    printf("Function called %d times\n", count);
}
```

Code Example Explanation

- count retains its value each time callCount is called, displaying the number of times it's been invoked.

Notes

Static variables are useful for tracking state information specific to a function.

Warnings

Static variables consume memory throughout the program's execution, so they should be used judiciously.

Relevant Project Section

Project Name

LED Toggle with Variable Scope Control

Project Goal

Use different types of variable scope to control an LED toggle frequency, demonstrating the persistence and accessibility of global, local, and static variables.

Requirement Components

- AVR Microcontroller (e.g., ATmega328P)
- LED connected to a GPIO pin

Component Connection Table

Component	Microcontroller Pin	Additional Notes
LED	PORTB0	Connect with a current-limiting resistor

Connection Analysis

The LED is connected to PORTB0 on the microcontroller. The program will toggle the LED using a function that relies on a static local variable for timing control, with a global variable to manage the LED state.

Program Software Setup

1. Open Atmel Studio and create a new project.
2. Configure PORTB0 as an output for controlling the LED.

3. Implement functions with local, global, and static variables to manage the LED toggle.

Project Code

```c
#include <avr/io.h>
#include <util/delay.h>

int ledState = 0;  // Global variable to track LED state (on/off)

// Function to initialize LED pin
void LED_init() {
    DDRB |= (1 << PORTB0);  // Set PORTB0 as output
}

// Function to toggle the LED state with a static delay counter
void LED_toggle() {
    static int delayCounter = 0;  // Static variable to persist delay value

    if (delayCounter >= 5) {  // Toggle every 5 calls
        ledState = !ledState;  // Update global variable to change LED state
        if (ledState) {
            PORTB |= (1 << PORTB0);  // Turn LED on
        } else {
            PORTB &= ~(1 << PORTB0);  // Turn LED off
        }
        delayCounter = 0;  // Reset static delay counter
    } else {
        delayCounter++;  // Increment delay counter
    }
}

int main(void) {
    LED_init();  // Initialize LED

    while (1) {
        LED_toggle();  // Call toggle function in loop
        _delay_ms(100);  // Delay to observe toggling effect
    }
}
```

Save and Run

1. Save and compile the code in Atmel Studio.
2. Upload the code to the microcontroller.

3. Observe the LED toggling every 500 ms (5 calls with a 100 ms delay each).

Check Output

- The LED should toggle on and off periodically, controlled by the LED_toggle function.
- The global variable ledState manages the LED state across function calls, while the static variable delayCounter persists between calls to control the toggle frequency.

Chapter-20 Memory Management and EEPROM

Chapter Overview

Memory management is critical in embedded systems programming, where resources are limited. AVR microcontrollers provide various memory types—program memory (Flash), data memory (SRAM), and EEPROM (Electrically Erasable Programmable Read-Only Memory). EEPROM is particularly valuable for storing data that needs to persist after a power cycle. This chapter will cover memory types, EEPROM functions, and practical examples for reading and writing to EEPROM, with an emphasis on when and why to use each type of memory effectively.

Chapter Goal

- Understand the different memory types in AVR microcontrollers and their specific uses.
- Learn to store and retrieve data from EEPROM, an essential feature for persistent data storage.
- Implement EEPROM read and write operations to manage non-volatile data storage effectively in embedded applications.

Rules

- **Program Memory (Flash)**: Stores the program code and constants and is non-volatile, meaning it retains data even when the microcontroller is powered off.
- **Data Memory (SRAM)**: Used for temporary storage of variables and data during runtime; it is volatile and loses data when powered off.
- **EEPROM**: Non-volatile memory that stores data that must persist across power cycles. Suitable for data that is read and written infrequently to avoid memory wear.
- **Memory Efficiency**: Efficient use of memory resources is critical in embedded programming to avoid wasting limited memory and to maintain system stability.

Brief Introduction to Memory Management

AVR microcontrollers are resource-constrained, making efficient memory management essential. They contain different types of memory, each with unique characteristics and intended uses:

- **Flash Memory** is used for program code storage and constant data.
- **SRAM** stores variables and runtime data but loses data when power is off.
- **EEPROM** provides non-volatile storage suitable for configuration settings, calibration values, and other persistent data. Knowing how to use each memory type helps optimize performance, manage power efficiency, and prevent data loss in embedded applications.

Memory Types in AVR Microcontrollers

1. Program Memory (Flash Memory)

What is Program Memory

Flash memory in AVR microcontrollers is a type of non-volatile memory that retains its content when the power is off. It is used to store the compiled program code and constants that do not change during program execution.

Use Purpose

- **Store Program Code**: Holds the application code that the microcontroller executes.
- **Hold Constant Data**: Stores constant values that do not change at runtime, such as look-up tables or text messages.

Characteristics

- **Non-Volatile**: Data is retained without power.
- **Limited Write Cycles**: Flash memory can be reprogrammed a limited number of times (usually between 10,000 to 100,000 cycles).
- **Read-Only at Runtime**: Flash memory can typically be read but not modified during runtime.

Syntax

```
const char text[] PROGMEM = "Hello, World!";
```

Syntax Explanation

- **const char text[]**: Declares a constant character array text.
- **PROGMEM**: Macro indicating that text is stored in Flash memory.

Simple Code Example

```
const char message[] PROGMEM = "Welcome to AVR!";
```

Code Example Explanation

- The string "Welcome to AVR!" is stored in Flash memory, making it accessible at runtime without occupying SRAM.

Notes
Using Flash memory for constant data saves SRAM space, which is essential for variables.

Warnings
Flash memory should not be used for frequently changing data due to limited write cycles.

---

2. Data Memory (SRAM)
What is Data Memory (SRAM)
SRAM (Static Random Access Memory) is volatile memory used for temporary data, such as variables, during program execution. SRAM is cleared when power is off.
Use Purpose
- **Store Variables**: Holds temporary variables that may change frequently during runtime.
- **Manage Stack and Heap**: Used for function call stacks, function parameters, and temporary values.

Characteristics

- **Volatile**: Loses data when the power is turned off.
- **Limited Size**: Typically smaller than Flash and EEPROM, so efficient usage is crucial.

Syntax

```
int runtimeValue = 42;
```

Syntax Explanation

- `int runtimeValue`: Declares an integer variable `runtimeValue` stored in SRAM, initialized to 42.

Simple Code Example

```
int counter = 0;
counter++;  // Updates the variable in SRAM
```

Code Example Explanation
- The variable `counter` is stored in SRAM and can be updated dynamically during runtime.

Notes
SRAM is valuable for holding variables that change during program execution but does not retain data after a power cycle.

Warnings
Running out of SRAM can cause stack overflow, resulting in crashes or unpredictable behavior. Efficient memory management is key.

---

3. EEPROM (Electrically Erasable Programmable Read-Only Memory)

What is EEPROM
EEPROM is a non-volatile memory that can retain data across power cycles. It is slower than SRAM and is intended for data that does not change frequently, such as user settings, calibration data, or data that must be retained permanently.

Use Purpose

- **Non-Volatile Data Storage**: Suitable for storing data like configuration settings or calibration values that must persist across reboots.
- **Updateable Data**: Can be modified during runtime, though writes should be minimized due to limited write cycles.

Characteristics

- **Non-Volatile**: Retains data without power.
- **Limited Write Cycles**: Typically around 100,000 write cycles; using the eeprom_update function helps avoid unnecessary writes.
- **Slower Access**: EEPROM access is slower than SRAM, so it should not be used for time-critical data.

Syntax

```
uint8_t savedValue = eeprom_read_byte((uint8_t*)0x00);
```

Syntax Explanation

- **uint8_t savedValue**: Declares a variable to store a byte read from EEPROM.
- **eeprom_read_byte**: Reads a byte from the specified EEPROM address.

Simple Code Example

```
eeprom_write_byte((uint8_t*)0x10, 0x55);   // Write 0x55 to EEPROM at
address 0x10
```

Code Example Explanation

- Writes the value 0x55 to EEPROM at address 0x10.

Notes

EEPROM memory is useful for data that needs to persist but does not change frequently.

EEPROM Functions and Usage Examples

1. EEPROM Read Byte

What is EEPROM Read Byte

The `eeprom_read_byte()` function reads a single byte from a specific address in EEPROM.

Syntax

```
uint8_t eeprom_read_byte(const uint8_t* addr);
```

Syntax Explanation

- **const uint8_t* addr**: Pointer to the EEPROM address to read from.
- **Returns**: The byte stored at the specified EEPROM address.

Simple Code Example

```
uint8_t value = eeprom_read_byte((uint8_t*)0x00);
```

Code Example Explanation

- Reads a byte from EEPROM address 0x00 and stores it in `value`.

---

2. EEPROM Write Byte

What is EEPROM Write Byte

The `eeprom_write_byte()` function writes a single byte to a specific EEPROM address.

Syntax

```
void eeprom_write_byte(uint8_t* addr, uint8_t val);
```

Syntax Explanation

- **uint8_t* addr**: Pointer to the EEPROM address to write to.
- **uint8_t val**: The value to be written.

Simple Code Example

```
eeprom_write_byte((uint8_t*)0x00, 42);
```

Code Example Explanation

- Writes the value 42 to EEPROM address 0x00.

---

3. EEPROM Update Byte

What is EEPROM Update Byte

The eeprom_update_byte() function only writes a byte if the current value differs from the new value, reducing unnecessary write cycles and extending EEPROM lifespan.

Syntax

```
void eeprom_update_byte(uint8_t* addr, uint8_t val);
```

Syntax Explanation

- **uint8_t* addr**: Pointer to the EEPROM address to update.
- **uint8_t val**: The new value to write if it differs from the current value.

Simple Code Example

```
eeprom_update_byte((uint8_t*)0x00, 42);
```

Code Example Explanation

- Updates the byte at address 0x00 with 42 only if it currently holds a different value.

---

4. EEPROM Read Block

What is EEPROM Read Block
The `eeprom_read_block()` function reads multiple bytes from EEPROM and stores them in an SRAM buffer.

Syntax

```
void eeprom_read_block(void* dest, const void* src, size_t n);
```

Syntax Explanation

- **`void* dest`**: Destination buffer in SRAM.
- **`const void* src`**: Source address in EEPROM.
- **`size_t n`**: Number of bytes to read.

Simple Code Example

```
uint8_t buffer[10];
eeprom_read_block(buffer, (const void*)0x00, 10);
```

Code Example Explanation

- Reads 10 bytes from EEPROM starting at address 0x00 and stores them in `buffer`.

---

5. EEPROM Write Block

What is EEPROM Write Block
The `eeprom_write_block()` function writes multiple bytes from an SRAM buffer to EEPROM.

Syntax

```
void eeprom_write_block(const void* src, void* dest, size_t n);
```

Syntax Explanation
- **`const void* src`**: Source buffer in SRAM.
- **`void* dest`**: Destination address in EEPROM.
- **`size_t n`**: Number of bytes to write.

Simple Code Example

```
uint8_t data[10] = {0, 1, 2, 3, 4, 5, 6, 7, 8, 9};
eeprom_write_block(data, (void*)0x00, 10);
```

Code Example Explanation

- Writes 10 bytes from data into EEPROM starting at address 0x00.

Relevant Project Section

Project Name
EEPROM Data Logging

Project Goal
Implement an EEPROM-based data logging program to store sensor readings in EEPROM and retrieve them after a reset or power cycle.

Requirement Components

- AVR Microcontroller (e.g., ATmega328P)
- Sensor (e.g., temperature or light sensor)

Component Connection Table

Component	Microcontroller Pin	Additional Notes
Sensor	ADC pin	Analog sensor for data logging

Connection Analysis
The sensor connects to an ADC pin on the microcontroller to read data values that are stored in EEPROM. The program reads values from EEPROM after a reset to demonstrate persistent data storage.

Program Software Setup
1. Open Atmel Studio and create a new project.
2. Configure ADC for reading sensor values.
3. Implement EEPROM read and write functions to store and retrieve sensor data.

Project Code

```c
#include <avr/io.h>
#include <avr/eeprom.h>
#include <util/delay.h>

#define SENSOR_ADDR (uint8_t*)0x00  // EEPROM address for storing
sensor data

void ADC_init() {
    ADMUX = (1<<REFS0);  // Set reference voltage
    ADCSRA = (1<<ADEN) | (1<<ADPS2) | (1<<ADPS1);  // Enable ADC and
set prescaler
}

uint16_t ADC_read() {
    ADCSRA |= (1<<ADSC);  // Start conversion
    while (ADCSRA & (1<<ADSC));  // Wait for conversion to complete
    return ADC;
}

int main(void) {
    ADC_init();
    uint8_t sensorData = (uint8_t)(ADC_read() >> 2);  // Scale to 8
bits
    eeprom_update_byte(SENSOR_ADDR, sensorData);  // Store sensor data
in EEPROM

    // Retrieve and output stored sensor data for demonstration
    uint8_t storedData = eeprom_read_byte(SENSOR_ADDR);
    // Simulated output (e.g., UART transmit for real system)
    while (1);
}
```

Save and Run

1. Save and compile the code in Atmel Studio.
2. Upload the code to the microcontroller.
3. Test by reading sensor data stored in EEPROM after a power cycle or reset.

Chapter-21 Power Management and Optimization

Chapter Overview

Power management is crucial in embedded systems, especially in battery-operated devices. AVR microcontrollers offer various techniques to manage and reduce power consumption, such as sleep modes, peripheral control, and clock scaling. These features enable developers to conserve energy and improve efficiency in embedded applications. This chapter will explore power management strategies and optimization techniques with practical examples to implement them.

Chapter Goal

- Understand the power management options available on AVR microcontrollers.
- Learn how to use sleep modes, peripheral control, and clock scaling to reduce power consumption.
- Implement power management techniques in a practical project for optimized power usage.

Rules

- **Sleep Modes**: Use sleep modes to reduce power consumption when the microcontroller is idle.
- **Peripheral Control**: Disable unused peripherals to avoid unnecessary power drain.
- **Clock Scaling**: Adjust the system clock to balance power savings and performance.
- **Code Optimization**: Use efficient coding practices to minimize resource use and power consumption.

Brief Introduction to Power Management in AVR Microcontrollers

AVR microcontrollers provide multiple features to optimize power consumption, including various sleep modes, peripheral control, and clock scaling. These techniques allow developers to manage power according to the performance needs of their applications, enhancing battery life and system efficiency. By leveraging these features, microcontroller-based devices can operate longer on the same power source, making power management essential for energy-efficient design.

Syntax Table

Serial No	Topic	Syntax	Example
1	Set Sleep Mode	`set_sleep_mode(SLEEP_MODE_TYPE);`	`set_sleep_mode(SLEEP_MODE_IDLE);`
2	Enable Sleep	`sleep_enable();`	`sleep_enable();`
3	Enter Sleep	`sleep_cpu();`	`sleep_cpu();`
4	Disable Sleep	`sleep_disable();`	`sleep_disable();`
5	Power Reduction (ADC)	PRR	= (1 << PRADC);
6	Power Reduction (Timer)	PRR	= (1 << PRTIM1);
7	Clock Prescaler	`clock_prescale_set(clock_div_x);`	`clock_prescale_set(clock_div_2);`

Power Management Techniques in AVR Microcontrollers

1. Sleep Modes

What are Sleep Modes

Sleep modes reduce power usage by selectively shutting down parts of the microcontroller. AVR microcontrollers support several sleep modes that progressively lower power consumption, from **Idle Mode** (minimal power savings) to **Power-Down Mode** (maximum power savings).

Use Purpose

- **Reduce Power Usage**: Minimizes power draw when the microcontroller is idle or in standby.
- **Increase Battery Life**: Essential for battery-powered applications, where long-term operation on limited power is required.

Available Sleep Modes

- **Idle Mode**: Halts the CPU but keeps peripherals (like timers) running, allowing for quick wake-up.
- **ADC Noise Reduction Mode**: Pauses the CPU while keeping the ADC running to improve analog-to-digital conversion accuracy.
- **Power-Down Mode**: The deepest sleep mode, disabling most functions except for wake-up sources like external interrupts.
- **Standby Mode**: Similar to Power-Down Mode but with quicker wake-up times.

Syntax

```
set_sleep_mode(SLEEP_MODE_TYPE);
sleep_enable();
sleep_cpu();
```

Syntax Explanation

- **`set_sleep_mode(SLEEP_MODE_TYPE);`**: Sets the microcontroller to the desired sleep mode (e.g., SLEEP_MODE_IDLE, SLEEP_MODE_PWR_DOWN).
- **`sleep_enable();`**: Enables sleep mode.
- **`sleep_cpu();`**: Activates the sleep mode, reducing power consumption until an interrupt wakes the microcontroller.

Simple Code Example

```c
#include <avr/sleep.h>

void enterIdleMode() {
    set_sleep_mode(SLEEP_MODE_IDLE);   // Set mode to Idle
    sleep_enable();
    sleep_cpu();   // Enters sleep until an interrupt occurs
    sleep_disable();   // Disable sleep on wake-up
}
```

Code Example Explanation

- This function configures the microcontroller to enter Idle Mode, halting the CPU but keeping peripherals active until an interrupt wakes it up.

Notes

Each sleep mode offers different levels of power savings and wake-up times. Choose the mode based on the system's performance requirements.

Warnings

Properly configure wake-up sources like interrupts; otherwise, the microcontroller may not wake up as expected.

---

2. Peripheral Control

What is Peripheral Control

Peripheral control allows developers to enable or disable specific peripherals, such as ADC, timers, or communication interfaces, to save power when they are not in use.

Use Purpose

- **Reduce Unnecessary Power Usage**: Save power by turning off peripherals that are temporarily unnecessary.
- **Optimize System Efficiency**: Enable peripherals only when required, reducing overall power consumption.

Peripheral Control Commands

- **ADC**: Disable the Analog-to-Digital Converter when analog reading is not needed.
- **Timers**: Disable timers not in use to lower power consumption.
- **Communication Interfaces**: Disable UART, SPI, or I2C if not required for the current operation.

Syntax

```
PRR |= (1 << PRADC);   // Disable ADC
PRR |= (1 << PRTIM1);  // Disable Timer1
```

Syntax Explanation

- **PRR**: The Power Reduction Register, which controls enabling/disabling various peripherals.
- **(1 << PRADC)**: Bit to disable the ADC.
- **(1 << PRTIM1)**: Bit to disable Timer1.

Simple Code Example

```
void disableUnusedPeripherals() {
    PRR |= (1 << PRADC);  // Disable ADC to save power
    PRR |= (1 << PRSPI);  // Disable SPI if unused
}
```

Code Example Explanation

- This function disables the ADC and SPI peripherals to conserve power.

Notes
Disabling peripherals conserves power, but they must be re-enabled when needed for correct operation.

Warnings
Ensure essential peripherals remain enabled to avoid unexpected functionality loss.

---

3. Clock Scaling (Clock Prescaler)

What is Clock Scaling
Clock scaling involves adjusting the microcontroller's clock frequency. By reducing the clock frequency, power consumption is decreased, but this also reduces processing speed.

Use Purpose

- **Balance Performance and Power Consumption**: Run the microcontroller at the necessary speed to save power.
- **Adaptive Power Management**: Scale down the clock during low-demand periods to optimize power usage.

Clock Prescaler Options

- The clock prescaler can be set to values like `clock_div_1`, `clock_div_2`, `clock_div_4`, etc., which divide the system clock accordingly.
- For example, `clock_div_2` reduces the clock speed to half its original frequency, reducing power consumption proportionally.

Syntax

```
clock_prescale_set(clock_div_x);
```

Syntax Explanation

- `clock_prescale_set()`: Function to set the clock prescaler.
- `clock_div_x`: The division factor (e.g., `clock_div_2` for half speed).

Simple Code Example

```
#include <avr/power.h>

void setClockToHalfSpeed() {
    clock_prescale_set(clock_div_2);   // Sets clock to half speed
}
```

Code Example Explanation

- This function sets the microcontroller's clock to half the
  maximum frequency, saving power during low-demand
  periods.

Notes
Reducing the clock frequency conserves power, but this may affect
the performance of time-critical operations.

Warnings
Ensure that the selected clock frequency meets the timing
requirements of peripherals, as slower clock speeds may affect their
operation.

Relevant Project Section

Project Name
Power-Efficient Temperature Logger

Project Goal
Implement a power-efficient temperature logging system using sleep
modes and peripheral control to minimize power consumption.

Requirement Components

- AVR Microcontroller (e.g., ATmega328P)
- Temperature sensor (e.g., LM35)
- LED for status indication

Component Connection Table

Component	Microcontroller Pin	Additional Notes
Temperature Sensor	ADC pin	Analog input for temperature
LED	PORTB0	Used to indicate active state

Connection Analysis

The temperature sensor connects to an ADC pin, while an LED on PORTB0 indicates the microcontroller's active state. The microcontroller reads the temperature at intervals, then enters sleep mode to conserve power between readings.

Program Software Setup

1. Open Atmel Studio and create a new project.
2. Configure ADC for reading temperature values.
3. Implement sleep mode and peripheral control for power management.

Project Code

```
#include <avr/io.h>
#include <avr/sleep.h>
#include <avr/power.h>
#include <util/delay.h>

#define LED_PIN PORTB0

void ADC_init() {
    ADMUX = (1 << REFS0);  // Set reference voltage to AVCC
    ADCSRA = (1 << ADEN) | (1 << ADPS2) | (1 << ADPS1);  // Enable ADC
and set prescaler
}

uint16_t ADC_read() {
    ADCSRA |= (1 << ADSC);  // Start conversion
    while (ADCSRA & (1 << ADSC));  // Wait for conversion to complete
    return ADC;
}

void enterSleepMode() {
```

```c
    set_sleep_mode(SLEEP_MODE_PWR_DOWN);  // Set sleep mode to power-
down
    sleep_enable();
    sleep_cpu();  // Enter sleep mode
    sleep_disable();  // Disable sleep mode after waking up
}

void setup() {
    DDRB |= (1 << LED_PIN);  // Set LED_PIN as output
    ADC_init();
}

int main(void) {
    setup();
    uint16_t temp_value;

    while (1) {
        PORTB |= (1 << LED_PIN);  // Turn on LED to indicate active
state
        temp_value = ADC_read();  // Read temperature from sensor
        _delay_ms(100);  // Brief delay for demonstration
        PORTB &= ~(1 << LED_PIN);  // Turn off LED

        // Enter sleep mode to save power until the next reading
        enterSleepMode();
    }
}
```

Save and Run

1. Save and compile the code in Atmel Studio.
2. Upload the code to the microcontroller.
3. Observe the LED indicator, which lights up during the temperature reading and turns off during sleep mode, indicating power-saving intervals.

Check Output

- The microcontroller reads the temperature value at intervals, conserving power by entering sleep mode between readings.
- The LED indicates when the microcontroller is active and turns off during sleep mode to save power.